Cochrane Shipbuilders
Vol 1 : 1884 - 1914

by

Tony Lofthouse, Gilbert Mayes,
David Newton, Michael Thompson

Andrew Cochrane senior, died 1917.

FOREWORD

To compile the history of a shipyard as prolific and diverse as Cochrane's has taken the authors many years of research. Numerous people have come forward to assist in the work including shipping historians, enthusiasts, archivists and librarians. To illustrate the book, photographs have been obtained from several notable collections. Representations are included of the house flags and funnels of prominent owners.

In the early years the shipyard was ideally placed for the rapid expansion of the Hull and Grimsby fishing industries as owners moved from sail to steam. The company flourished as it took full advantage of this opportunity. Although the main business of the shipyard continued in advancing the construction of trawlers, there was a gradual progression to the inclusion of drifters, tugs and coasters.

Volume One takes the reader from the origins up to the beginning of the Great War and includes details of vessels taken into Admiralty service. The book provides an insight into the advances in design which trawler owners were constantly seeking in order to improve the catching ability of their fleets.

Michael Thompson, Hull, November 2012

ACKNOWLEDGEMENTS

Ken Marshall, the Managing Director of Cochrane's when it finally ceased operations, and naval architect Eric Hammall clarified numerous questions which arose out of a study of the Cochrane archives and provided additional details from their own memories and experience of the yard.

Arthur Credland, former Keeper of the Hull Maritime Museum, organised the Cochrane archive and assembled the outline history of the company.

John Freeman undertook genealogical investigations which provided key information about Andrew Cochrane's origins in Scotland and his partners Hamilton, Cooper and Schofield during the early period at Selby.

Derek Grindell illuminated the early days at Grovehill by his searches in the Beverley archive.

Ann Cowne, information administrator at Lloyd's Register of Shipping, London, provided assistance with researching changes of owners and names, and vessels lost and broken up.

Brian Egan helped in researching Lloyd's Register of Shipping, London.

Jonathan Grobler (Grimsby Trawlers) and Paul Whiting (George Scales' collection) provided additional photographs.

Bill Blow produced the information about house flags and funnel colours.

The staff of Hull History Centre and of the Hull Central Library gave assistance with registers, company ledgers and newspapers.

Publications including *Lloyd's Register, Customs House Registration folios, Mercantile Navy Lists* and *Olsen's Fisherman's nautical Almanack.*

Last and certainly not least, the authors wish to thank the staff of 4Word in Bristol for the pre-press work and Small Run Press for the splendid printing.

Published by Bernard McCall, 400 Nore Road, Portishead, Bristol, BS20 8EZ, England.
Website : www.coastalshipping.co.uk.   Telephone/fax : 01275 846178. Email : bernard@coastalshipping.co.uk.
All distribution enquiries should be addressed to the publisher.

Printed by Short Run Press, 25 Bittern Road, Exeter, EX2 7LW.
Telephone : 01392 211909.   Fax: 01392 444134.   Email: info@shortrunpress.co.uk.

ISBN : 978-1-902953-59-5

Cochrane's of Beverley and Selby

Andrew Cochrane, born 1840 at Glasserton, Wigtownshire, came south from Scotland after gaining experience in his home country. His birthplace was in southern Galloway not too far from Stranraer where no doubt his father had come ashore on the ferry from Ireland. Aged 16, he started an apprenticeship on 9 June 1856 in Dumbarton, on the Clyde, probably at one or other of the two long-established shipyards there, William Denny (1844) or A MacMillan (1834). In 1861 the census returns show that Cochrane was living at Dunglass, Old Kilpatrick, and he was described as a journeyman ship carpenter. Between Old Kilpatrick and Dumbarton is Bowling, once the location of the famous yard of Scott and Sons. Listed in the 1871 census as a ship carpenter, he was living with his wife and family in Dumbarton and we know that he was an under foreman shipwright at Napiers circa 1875-1877 and an under foreman carpenter in 1878-1879 at Alexander Stephen and Son, Linthouse, Govan, on Clydeside. A character reference from the latter states 'The bearer Andrew Cochrane has been in our employment as an under foreman carpenter for about two years. We found him an intelligent, trustworthy and pushing foreman. He leaves us of his own accord to fill a better situation' (20 Nov 1879)[1].

The 1881 census records Andrew Cochrane, ship carpenter, and his wife as living at 7 Belvedere Terrace, Southcoates. There were three children: Andrew aged 15, Jesse aged 13, and Maggie Jane. By 1884 he and the family were living in Grovehill Road, Beverley. He was working at the Vulcan Ironworks and when this closed in the same year he persuaded a fellow Scot (from Renfrew), Andrew Hamilton, who was also working at the yard, to join him in establishing a new shipbuilding company on the site. George Cooper, born in Ashton-under-Lyne in 1852, was also employed at the Vulcan yard. A friend of Hamilton, he was persuaded to join them. It is probable that all three had initially been attracted to Yorkshire to work at Earle's shipyard [2], Hull's biggest shipbuilding enterprise which built a huge diversity of craft, from trawlers to warships. We know that Cochrane was living at Southcoates in 1881, Hamilton, a boilermaker, at Drypool in the same year and Cooper, a foreman riveter, at 16 Craven Street, Southcoates.

A Mr Gemmell[3] of Hull made the design for Cochrane's first production, the **Albion of York**, and this is presumably William M Gemmell, born in Port Glasgow in 1847, who had been apprenticed to C and W Earle. He, along with W J Cook and C K Welton, set up his own yard in Hull which launched its first vessel in January 1885[4].

The site at Grovehill, Beverley, on the west bank of the River Hull, had became available with the premature demise of the Vulcan Ironworks Co Ltd. Formerly Fowler and McCollin of the Vulcan Ironworks Scott Street, Hull who in 1848 described themselves as engineers, millwrights, iron and brass founders, boiler makers, general smiths, etc. Later, circa 1863, there were also works in Wincolmlee and at the Navigation Iron Works, Railway Dock Side. They evidently were reformed as the Vulcan Ironworks Co, Hull, Ltd, under which name they appear in the catalogue of the 1883 International Fisheries Exhibition, London, describing themselves as mechanical engineers, boiler makers, engine builders, brass and iron founders, millwrights, iron shipbuilders, agricultural implement manufacturers, oil mill machinery, etc. Presumably the restructuring was directly linked to the setting up of the yard at Beverley.

The Town Clerk of Beverley sent a letter to the Vulcan Iron Works Co, dated 24 August 1882, with a draft of a proposed lease (BC/IV/9/4P.359, Beverley Archives). The application to rent a paddock at Grovehill, then in the occupation of Mr Thomas Harrison, was considered by the Beverley Corporation in September 1882[5] and by 16th of the month Harrison had surrendered his tenancy and by October the agreement was completed with Vulcan whose intention it was to build an iron screw steamer 230 feet long. The Corporation was to receive rent from the land and the advantage of Beck dues during an estimated eight month completion time. Vulcan were to be there for a trial period of twelve months and continue thereafter if the venture was successful. Rent for the first year would be £20, £15 for second year, and £10 for the third and subsequent years. The estimated wages bill for wages was £5,000 (presumably for a year) and material to the value of £1,000 to be purchased locally would have given a tremendous boost to the Beverley economy. By December the Vulcan Ironworks were tenants of three gardens and ground in occupation of Tigars Manure works[6].

Directly opposite on the east bank was the yard of Joseph Scarr. He and his kin had establishments here, also at Beckside, Beverley, and later at Hessle Haven[7]. Established in 1882, Vulcan built Beverley's first iron vessel, the **Fawn**, which was ready for launch on 9 June 1883 (*Beverley Guardian*, 9 June 1883). A reply dated 8 June from the Town Clerk of Beverley declined an invitation to attend the launch because of the state of his health. The *Beverley Guardian*, 16 June 1883, has a lengthy article entitled 'The new iron shipyard at Grovehill'.

'It having been announced that the first iron ship built by the Vulcan Ironworks Company at Grovehill, would be launched on Saturday morning last, there was gathered together, as might naturally be expected, a very large concourse of people, eager to see the monster vessel take the water. To give those of our readers who have not seen the ship an idea of her dimensions, we may state that its length is 230 feet between the perpendiculars, breadth 32 feet, and depth of hold to Lloyd's floor line, 15ft. 6.5in. Her carrying capacity is 1,400 tons dead weight gross tonnage 1150 — The vessel has been constructed under the direction of Mr Wood, general manager of the company, Mr Drumlin, marine superintendent, and Mr McLintock, the manager of the Grovehill works. Such is the description of the ship, to see the launching of which broadside into the river Hull, caused such an assembly of people, numbering thousands, at Grovehill on Saturday morning. The occasion was made on of considerable rejoicing, and flags were freely displayed from houses on the road and from various parts of the works. A platform had been erected by Mr T Harrison, outside the Nag's Head, from which a good view of the launch could be seen, and this was crowded with spectators as was also every elevated piece of ground near. A couple of barges lying across the river, and the banks on either side also swarmed with people. A temporary bridge was thrown over the river for the convenience of those wishing to see the launch from the opposite bank. A staging had been erected immediately behind the vessel for the accommodation of the directors and those who were to take part in the ceremony, and upon it were Z T Welburn, Esq, of Scarboro' (chairman of the Company), Miss Welburn, the Mayor of Beverley and Mrs E Crosskill, Mr J.Lee and Mr T Lee of Gardham (directors of the Company), Mrs J Lee, the Rev G C Fisher, the Rev W C Barnard, the Rev R Shepherd, Mr and Mrs George Jackson, and Mr Walter Jackson, of London, Mr and Mrs Taite of Bridlington, and others.'

Unfortunately it was twelve days later when she finally entered the water. Clearly it was a challenge launching into a relatively narrow river but both Beverley and Selby shipyards were later to perfect the art of broadside launching, an impressive spectacle, with a mighty splash followed by a miniature 'tidal wave' up the banks. The same article in the *Beverley Guardian* contains a report of the after-dinner speech of Z T Welburn who reveals that it 'was their idea first to go to Goole, but the Corporation of Beverley met them in such an amicable manner that they were induced to enter an agreement with them, and he hoped they should never regret it.'

The Tom Harrison, born in 1837, who erected one of the stands was a journeyman ship carpenter and also the landlord of the Nags Head, located on the west bank of the river Hull at the ferry crossing. Mrs Crosskill was no doubt part of the family of founders and manufacturers of agricultural machinery active in Beverley until 1864. There had been loss of employment following the closure of the Iron and Wagon Co and it was hoped by the town worthies and the citizens that the Vulcan yard, and Henry and Joseph Scarr's Iron Works at Beck End already established, would provide employment for significant numbers of men.

The **Fawn** was the first of four iron ships for Messrs Jacksons to be launched at Grovehill, the 100 hp engines to be made and fitted at Hull. Mrs Jackson named the vessel **Fawn** and the launch party had to leave her stuck in the mud to have luncheon at the Telegraph Inn. Messrs Jacksons took receipt of an identical vessel and two other smaller craft[8].

On Tuesday morning the sister ship **Roebuck** was named by Rose Jackson, daughter of one of the owners and only 10 to 12 years old, but could not be launched and the assembly retired to the Kings Arms Hotel to celebrate[9]; Lt Col Young of the Londesborough Estate was present at the luncheon. The vessel was finally launched on the Thursday evening at midnight.

The Vulcan Ironworks received the accolade of a silver medal at the International Fisheries Exhibition for a capstan engine and exhibited there a model of the **Fawn**[10]. On Thursday, November 1883, the **Wild Rose** was launched at 9.30am by Miss Hobson, daughter of John Hobson of York, for the York - Hull passenger/cargo trade. The vessel was 84 feet long, 17.9 feet beam and 150 tons with 24hp surface condensing engines of Vulcan manufacture[11]. They leased more land for extensions to the yard including a sawmill and it is also recorded that a party of gentlemen 'said to be from Liverpool' also purchased land a little below the Vulcan works for the purpose of establishing a yard too. The fourth vessel, the **Hugin**, was launched by Mrs McLintock, wife of the shipyard manager for Mr Jacob Olson of Bergen.

These were not however the first iron ships to be built in Beverley for in November 1882 Henry and Joseph Scarr had launched an iron steamer into Beverley Beck. Because of its size, 115ft long, 17ft 9in beam and 9ft 9in depth, it was launched a few hundred yards downstream from the Navigation Iron Works, which was at the head of the Beck. The 35hp engine was built by Messrs Good and Menzies of Hull (*Beverley Guardian*, 18 Nov 1882). The report tells us that a few weeks earlier another iron vessel, somewhat smaller but undoubtedly Beverley's first, had been launched and purchased by Crathorne's, millers, who occupied a site at Grovehill.

By the end of the month the Vulcan yard was in serious financial difficulties and needed £900 for the next pay day. The Chancery Division moved for provisional liquidation of the Vulcan Ironworks while a local banking company, the biggest creditor, was prepared to advance money for paying the men[12]. The last vessel left Grovehill in December, the hands were paid off and the works closed[13]. All the mechanical plant and tools were sold by auction over two days in the following spring (*Beverley Guardian*, 22 March 1884). A creditors' meeting was held at the Imperial Hotel in Hull on 12 July when liabilities were announced to be £30,500. 18s. 6d and assets £10,194. 2s. 6d. After the disposal of the shipyard, the Hull works carried on at a profit (£200 in two months) and the creditors were advised to carry on supporting the firm, to which C D Holmes, the well-known engineer, agreed. It is not clear whether he was present as a creditor, part of the management, or possibly as an independent adviser[14].

Fowler and McCollin are listed in the Hull trade directory for 1885 at South Side, St Andrews Dock, but no further trace of the company can be discovered. In 1892 Tindall and Co were at the Vulcan Ironworks, Scott Street.

Thomas Crust, Beverley Town Clerk, wrote to Cochrane on 17 March 1884 saying 'I am directed by the Property Committee to acknowledge the receipt of your letter to the chairman and to say the only reply the Comm. give at present is that when the Grovehill Shipyard is to let by the Corp. you shall have the first offer' and on 28 April a lease was forwarded[15]. Already, the same month, Andrew Cochrane, who had purchased some of the Vulcan equipment, had begun preparing the site for building two fishing smacks. He had a nine year lease on the same conditions and rent as his predecessors[16]. A note in the local newspaper indicates that Cochrane and some at least of his partners had previously worked for Vulcan and hence of course would be have inside knowledge of the state of Vulcan; and 'Those who a few months ago were workmen in the yard had now become owners of the firm'[17]. A twin screw lighter, the **Albion of York**, christened by Mrs Cochrane and intended for the York - Goole trade, was launched in September 1884 for T F Ward and Co of York and had a 30hp engine by Fowler and McCollin. Converted to a dumb barge in 1940 for Frederick Hall of Hull, she was photographed afloat and in use at Goole in 1965 (see page 16).

After **Albion of York** there followed three iron-hulled smacks also designed by Gemmell for Robert Hellyer of Hull. The **Alpha** was launched by Mrs Hamilton, the **Beta** by Mrs Cooper, and the **Grovehill** by Mrs J Schofield. After the launch of the **Alpha**, invited guests took light refreshment in the mould loft and Alderman Hind said a few words giving a historical perspective to shipbuilding in Beverley and remarking that the **Isabella** used by Captain Ross for his North West Passage attempt in 1818 was built there (*Beverley Guardian*, 27 September 1884). Though this was based on a misunderstanding; an **Isabella** (97ft) was launched at Grovehill on 15 March 1803, but the whaler and exploration ship of that name, a vessel of 110ft, is simply described as being built on the River Hull, probably at Hull rather than Beverley. He further intimated 'that Messrs Cochrane, Hamilton and Cooper were not satisfied with their present enterprise, but were negotiating with a firm in London for sending out ships to the colonies, and he hoped they would succeed in doing so. They were at present turning over about £1000 a month, and he thought if they got 20% on that they would be getting a good profit. He then proposed the health of Mr Gemmell, of Hull, who had acted as draughtsman for the firm'.

STAFFA	18	145	100.8	C D Holmes	Christopher Pickering &
93147 Steam trawler	09.08.1888	67	20.5	45 nhp	Samuel L Haldane,
H49	10.09.1888		10.5	10.0 knots	Hull

10.09.1888: Registered at Hull (H49). 09.11.1889: Sold to W Bade & Co, Geestmünde, Germany.
09.11.1889: Hull registry closed. 1896: Renamed **POSEIDON** (PG23). 1900: Sold to J Von Eitzen, Altona, Germany.
1905: Sold to Gadus Fabriker, Gothenburg, Sweden. 1907: Renamed **KAROLINA**.
11.11.1916: Foundered following a collision whilst fishing approximately 9 miles east of Scaw Lightship.

IONA	19	145	100.8	C D Holmes	Christopher Pickering &
93150 Iron built steam	22.09.1888	67	20.5	45 nhp	Samuel L Haldane,
H51 trawler	27.10.1888		10.5	10.0 knots	Hull

27.10.1888: Registered at Hull (H51). 11.05.1889: Sold to Cia Portugezade de Pescaria, Lisbon, Portugal; renamed **HENRIQUE**.
14.06.1889: Hull registry closed. 08.10.1891: Wrecked whilst fishing approximately 15 miles north of Oporto.

WILD ROSE	20				Vessel contemplated but
					not built.

NILE	21	130	100.8	C D Holmes	William Wolfe & others,
95774 Iron built steam	22.10.1888	56	20.3	50 nhp 3-cyl	Hull
H54 trawler	11.1888		10.5	10.0 knots	

30.11.1888: Registered at Hull (H54). 01.06.1894: Wrecked off Iceland. 28.06.1894: Hull registry closed.

ULYSSES	22	157	106.5	C D Holmes	Grimsby Union Steam
96191 Iron built steam	18.02.1889	74	20.5	50 nhp 3-cyl	Fishing Co Ltd,
GY198 trawler	23.03.1889		11.5	10.0 knots	Grimsby

22.03.1889: Registered at Grimsby (GY198). 09.1898: Sold to Frederick H Brown, Grimsby.
01.1915: Requisitioned for war service for patrol duties (1-3 pdr) (Ad.No.1047). 11.07.1916: Renamed **ULYSSES II**.
11.1918: Returned and reverted to **ULYSSES** (GY198). 04.1924: Sold to L Stokka, Sandness, Norway, and renamed **JUSTI**.
Re-measured to 107.3' x 20.4'; tonnages amended to 174grt, 80net. 1928: Sold to D/S A/S Justi, Haugesund.
1930: Sold to Karl Soraas, Bergen. 1938: Sold to Math Michelsenanglelvik, Bergen. 1939: Sold to Ole R Rönneberg, Bergen.
1942: Sold to E S Stokka, Sandness. 1947: Sold to A/S Röykenes, Haugesund.
1956: Re-engined (2-stroke 4-cyl Alpha by Frederikshavn Jernst; engine made 1947).
1964: Sold to Brodrene Anda, Norway, for breaking up. 22.04.1964: Arrived at Stavanger. Broken up.

ROB ROY	23	149	105.7	C D Holmes	Christopher Pickering &
95810 Iron built steam	12.09.1889	71	20.3	45 ihp 2-cyl	Samuel L Haldane,
H80 trawler	17.10.1889		10.9	10.0 knots	Hull

15.10.1889: Registered at Hull (H80). 18.08.1891: Transferred to Pickering & Haldane's Steam Trawling Co Ltd, Hull.
31.10.1906: Sold to R Turnbull, Hartlepool. 10.1911: Sold to Collie, Aberdeen. 26.10.1911: Hull registry closed.
30.11.1911: Registered at Aberdeen (A417). 26.09.1912: Foundered 20 miles off Aberdeen following a collision in dense fog with
trawler **CARLTON** (GY270) (267grt/1907) (see Yard No. 388); nine crew took to boat and picked up by **CARLTON**. Landed at
Aberdeen. 09.08.1912: Aberdeen registry closed.

GOELAND	24	145	101.2	C D Holmes	Liverpool Steam Fishing
96384 Iron built steam	26.10.1889	63	20.3	45 ihp 3-cyl	Co Ltd,
LL110 trawler	26.11.1889		11.0	10.0 knots	Liverpool

25.11.1889: Registered at Liverpool (LL110). 1908: Sold to Cia De Pesca, Nav, Talcahuno, Chile. Liverpool registry closed.
Renamed **DON VINCENTE**. 1917: Sold to F C Sievers & Co, Coquimbo, and renamed **GERDA**.
1919: Vessel removed from Lloyd's Register of Shipping.

POCHARD	25	146	101.4	C D Holmes	Liverpool Steam Fishing
96393 Iron built steam	25.11.1889	63	20.3	45 rhp 3-cyl	Co Ltd,
LL112 trawler	25.12.1889		11.0	10.0 knots	Liverpool

20.12.1889: Registered at Liverpool (LL112). 12.1908: Sold to T Lauder, Aberdeen. 12.1908: Liverpool registry closed.
14.12.1908: Registered at Aberdeen (A250). 06.1917: Sold to R Clarke, Grimsby. 20.06.1917: Aberdeen registry closed.
23.06.1917: Registered at Grimsby (GY1069). 29.05.1917: Requisitioned for Fishery Reserve.
28.06.1918: Mined in the North Sea. No survivors. 19.07.1918: Grimsby registry closed.

AZALEA	26	165	106.4	C D Holmes	North Eastern Steam
96193 Iron built liner	1889	70	20.5	50 nhp 3-cyl	Fishing Co Ltd,
GY199 well fishing vsl	22.04.1889		11.5	10.0 knots	Grimsby

17.04.1889: Registered at Grimsby (GY199)
29.06.1897: Stranded in dense fog on the NW coast of Stroma, Orkney. 07.1897: Grimsby registry closed.

BEGONIA	27	165	106.5	C D Holmes	North Eastern Steam
96197 Iron built liner	16.05.1889	70	20.5	50 nhp 3-cyl	Fishing Co Ltd,
GY210 well fishing vsl	06.06.1889		11.5	10.0 knots	Grimsby

03.06.1889: Registered at Grimsby (GY210). 04.03.1908: Vessel wrecked on Sow & Pigs Rocks, north of Blyth.
03.04.1908: Grimsby registry closed.

CINERARIA	28	154	100.6	C D Holmes	North Eastern Steam
96201 Iron built steam	1889	71	20.7	50 nhp 3-cyl	Fishing Co Ltd,
GY216 trawler	08.1889		11.0	10.0 knots	Grimsby

06.08.1889: Registered at Grimsby (GY216).   18.07.1915: Missing while on a North Sea trip. No survivors.
07.09.1915: Grimsby registry closed - "Missing".

DAHLIA	29	155	100.9	C D Holmes	North Eastern Steam
96206 Iron built steam	31.07.1889	71	20.6	50 nhp 3-cyl	Fishing Co Ltd,
GY223 trawler	08.1889		11.0	10.0 knots	Grimsby

31.08.1889: Registered at Grimsby (GY223).   01.1915: Requisitioned for war service as a patrol vessel (1-6pdr) (Ad.No.731).
11.10.1915: Renamed **DAHLIA II** (GY223).   07.1918: Returned.   11.1919: North Eastern Steam Fishing Co Ltd in voluntary
liquidation.   12.1919: Sold to Thomas W Baskcomb, Grimsby.   20.03.1922: Renamed **DAHLIA** (GY223).
10.1935: Fleet of Thomas W Baskcomb sold to Fred Parkes, Blackpool.
11.1935: Sold to Consolidated Fisheries Ltd, Grimsby, and transferred to Lowestoft.   27.11.1935: Grimsby registry closed.
29.11.1935: Registered at Lowestoft (LT109).   1938: Sold to shipbreakers at Willebroek, Belgium, for breaking up.
20.08.1938: Lowestoft registry closed.   06.10.1938: Sailed Lowestoft for Belgium.

GENERAL GORDON	30	153	105.6	C D Holmes	Pickering & Haldane's
95819 Iron built steam	24.12.1889	72	20.3	50 nhp 3-cyl	Steam Trawling Co Ltd,
H88 trawler	07.02.1890		11.0	10.0 knots	Hull

07.02.1890: Registered at Hull (H88).   24.03.1890: Sold to George Henry Pile, London.
19.04.1890: Hull registry closed. Sold to owners in Portugal and removed from Lloyd's Register of Shipping.

UNA	31	155	101.0	C D Holmes	Grimsby Union Steam
96214 Iron built steam	08.02.1890	80	20.6	50 nhp 3-cyl	Fishing Co Ltd,
GY238 liner	01.03.1890		11.0	10.0 knots	Grimsby

04.03.1890: Registered at Grimsby (GY238).   10.1901: Sold to J W Bateman, Grimsby.
01.1904: Sold to J W Bateman, Fremantle, Western Australia.   18.01.1904: Grimsby registry closed.
01.1904: Registered at Fremantle, Western Australia. Lengthened to 111.0ft; tonnages amended to 178grt, 87net.
1908: Sold to J Lynn Ltd, Fremantle, Western Australia.   1917: Sold to The Government of Western Australia, Perth, Western
Australia.   1919: Sold to Irvin & Johnson (Cape Town) Ltd, Cape Town, South Africa.
1931: Scuttled off Cape Town to form an artificial reef.

HELEN McGREGOR	32	156	101.5	C D Holmes	Pickering & Haldane's
95830 Iron built steam	1890	52	20.6	45 nhp 2-cyl	Steam Trawling Co Ltd,
H94 trawler	21.05.1890		11.0	10.0 knots	Hull

19.05.1890: Registered at Hull (H94).   01.01.1904: Tonnage altered to 61net.   13.11.1906: Sold to R Turnbull, Hartlepool.
11.1911: Sold to Thomas Lauder, Aberdeen.   28.11.1911: Hull registry closed.   30.11.1911: Registered at Aberdeen (A420).
1914: Sold to N Ahlner, Smögen, Sweden.   27.07.1914: Aberdeen registry closed.   Renamed **THOR**.
1923: Sold to Fiskeri A/B Thor, Gothenburg.   01.1929: Sold to Gísli Magnússon, Vestmannaeyjar, Iceland.
28.01.1929: Renamed **OSKAR** (VE286).   15.10.1930: Stranded on Lundey Island in Skagafjörður, Iceland. All crew rescued by
another fishing vessel.

ANGUS	33	129	92.5	C D Holmes	S Waddington,
93409 Iron built steam	10.03.1890	43	20.0	35 nhp 2-cyl	Boston
BN7 trawler	12.04.1890		11.0	9.5 knots	

18.04.1890: Registered at Boston (BN7).   1903: Sold to S C Hall, Boston.   1908: Sold to T Olufsen, Durban, South Africa.
1908: Sold to C P Perks, Durban.   23.04.1908: Vessel wrecked at Bird Island, Algoa Bay, Western Cape, South Africa.

INDIA	34	169	119.5	C D Holmes	Hull Steam Fishing & Ice
95836 Iron built steam	17.05.1890	64	21.0	50 nhp 3-cyl	Co Ltd,
H68 trawler	18.06.1890		11.0	10.0 knots	Hull

23.06.1890: Registered at Hull (H68).   19.05.1894: Re-registered. Lengthened to 120.0ft; tonnages amended to 193grt, 88net.
27.12.1915: Sold to Peter Class & David James Boates (also recorded as Baxter), Grimsby.   03.01.1916: Hull registry closed.
07.01.1916: Registered at Grimsby (GY833).   10.1916: Sold to Alick Black, Grimsby.
29.05.1917: Requisitioned for Fishery Reserve.   1919: Released.
11.1926: Sold for breaking up.   10.11.1926: Grimsby registry closed.

MALTA	35	169	106.4	C D Holmes	Hull Steam Fishing & Ice
95840 Iron built steam	05.06.1890	64	21.0	50 nhp 3-cyl	Co Ltd,
H101 trawler	15.07.1890		11.0	10.0 knots	Hull

15.07.1890: Registered at Hull (H101).   27.09.1894: Re-registered (lengthened to 120.0ft, tonnages amended to195grt, 99net).
08.10.1907: Foundered following a collision in the North Sea.   26.10.1907: Hull registry closed.

FLY	36	158	101.4	C D Holmes	British Steam Trawling
95843 Iron built steam	03.07.1890	59	21.6	45 rhp 3-cyl	Co Ltd,
H104 trawler	21.08.1890		11.0	10.0 knots	Hull

30.08.1890: Registered at Hull (H104).   02.11.1912: Sold to James A Robertson, Fleetwood.   15.11.1912: Hull registry closed.
16.11.1912: Registered at Fleetwood (FD166).   07.12.1912: Sold to Active Fishing Co Ltd, Fleetwood.
01.01.1914: Tonnage amended to 60.23net.   29.05.1917: Requisitioned for Fishery Reserve.   1919: Released.
07.02.1920: Sold to Sydney M Cannon, Aberdeen.   20.02.1920: Fleetwood registry closed.
28.02.1920: Registered at Aberdeen (A284).   1924: Sold for breaking up.   26.09.1924: Aberdeen registry closed.

Cochrane & Cooper, Grovehill Shipyard, Beverley

HUGELIA	75	153	102.5	C D Holmes	North Eastern Steam
99682 Iron built steam	22.09.1892	67	20.5	50 nhp 3-cyl	Fishing Co Ltd,
GY472 trawler	26.10.1892		11.1	10.0 knots	Grimsby

22.10.1892: Registered at Grimsby (GY472). 06.1912: Sold to Consolidated Whaling & Deep Sea Fishing Co of South Africa Ltd, London. 19.02.1913: Stranded on rocks 5 miles W of Keiskamma River, Cape of Good Hope.
10.04.1913: Grimsby registry closed.

ALICE ISABEL	76	128	92.0	C D Holmes	James Schofield,
99686 Iron built steam	04.02.1893	59	20.5	40 nhp 2-cyl	Grimsby
GY480 trawler	09.03.1893		10.6	9.5 knots	

10.03.1893: Registered at Grimsby (GY480). 21.12.1894: Posted missing. No survivors. 17.01.1895: Grimsby registry closed.

WHITE ROSE	77	67	81.0	Vulcan Co	John Hobson,
99563 Iron built steam	1892	31	15.6	20 nhp 3-cyl	Hull
GY480 lighter	12.05.1892		7.6	9.0 knots	

12.05.1892: Registered at Hull. 30.09.1905: Sold to The South & West Yorkshire Trading Co Ltd, Hull.
15.05.1907: Sold to The Grimsby Express Packet Co Ltd, Grimsby. 30.09.1930: Hull registry closed.

N.E. LIGHTER	78	100	60.0		North Eastern Railway
	1892		16.5	N/A	Co Ltd
Lighter	25.04.1892				

N.E. LIGHTER	79	100	60.0		North Eastern Railway
	1892		16.5	N/A	Co Ltd
Lighter	19.05.1892				

MOYO	80	45	35.0		G R Sanderson & Co Ltd
	1892		10.6	N/A	
Water boat	18.05.1892				

METIS	81	36	35.0		G R Sanderson & Co Ltd
	1892		10.6	N/A	
Water boat	18.05.1892				

TUBULAR	82	117	94.0	C D Holmes	Tubular Twin Screw
99582 Iron built twin	12.09.1892	54	18.5	12 nhp 4-cyl	Amidships Propulsion Co Ltd,
screw cargo lighter	13.10.1892		7.9	9.0 knots	Scarborough

10.11.1892: Registered at Hull. 10.06.1899: Sold to Alexander F Burke, Dundee.
10.06.1899: Hull registry closed. Registered at Dundee. 15.12.1899: Stranded at New Biggin Point, Blyth, on passage from Middlesbrough towards Methil (wind south-easterly force 5). Vessel declared a total loss. 01.1900: Dundee registry closed.

NAIAD	83		35.0	C D Holmes	
	1893		10.5		
Water boat					

HOWDENSHIRE	84	162	100.7	C D Holmes	George Herbert Anderton,
99588 Iron built steam	20.12.1892	88	20.2	29 nhp 4-cyl	York
cargo lighter	14.01.1893		8.8	9.0 knots	

13.01.1893: Registered at Hull. 09.05.1899: Sold to Cuthbert Young, London. 11.05.1899: Hull registry closed.
11.05.1899: Sold to Solache Y Llanos, Gijon, Spain, and renamed VIVERO. 29.03.1908: Wrecked at Gijon.

OREGON	85	163	106.0	C D Holmes	Thomas Hamling & others,
99597 Iron built steam	26.03.1893	62	21.0	59 nhp 3-cyl	Hull
H213 trawler	1893		11.0		

01.06.1893: Registered at Hull (H213). 22.01.1894: Sold to Thomas Hamling & Co Ltd.
03.1906: Sold to Soc Anon Pesquera Gallega, Ferrol, Spain. 12.03.1906: Hull registry closed. Registered at Ferrol.
1917: Sold to Javier Arcelus, San Sebastián. Renamed KÁMENTXO. Registered at San Sebastián.
1919: Sold to Pesquera Malagueña S A, Malaga. 1920: Renamed PUNTA CALABURRA. Registered at Malaga.
1929: Sold to José Monis Garcia, Huelva. 05.02.1933: Wrecked at Mogador.

RHINE	86	117	88.4	C D Holmes	George F Sleight,
99702 Iron built steam	04.07.1893	36	20.1	44 nhp 2-cyl	Grimsby
GY518 trawler	27.07.1893		10.7	10.0 knots	

27.07.1893: Registered at Grimsby (GY518). 25.08.1914: Vessel sunk by German torpedo boat when fishing in the North Sea; crew taken prisoner. 09.11.1914: Grimsby registry closed - "Blown up by enemy".

RHONE 99704 Iron built steam GY521 trawler	87 1893 10.08.1893	117 36	88.4 20.1 10.7	C D Holmes 44 nhp 2-cyl	George F Sleight, Grimsby

14.08.1893: Registered at Grimsby (GY521). 1912: New boiler fitted. 12.1914: Requisitioned for war service (1-3pdr) (Ad.No.658).
7.1918: Returned. 10.1920: Sold to A Walker, Aberdeen. 25.10.1920: Grimsby registry closed.
17.11.1920: Registered at Aberdeen (A557). 1926: Sold to Chalutiers Gruenais Jourdain & Co, Dieppe, France.
02.02.1926: Aberdeen registry closed. Renamed **MONT DOL**. Re-measured to 26,49m x 5,94m x 3,2m (86.9' x 19.5' x 10.6');
tonnages amended to 120grt, 27net. 1927: Renamed **MARCEAU–JEAN**. 1928: Sold to Ildevert Dupuis, Dieppe.
1932: Sold to Soc De Récupérations Sous-Marines, La Rochelle. 29.05.1934: Foundered off Barfleur.

CAMENES 93078 Iron built steam H1494 trawler	88 1886 1886	153 79	98.8 20.0 11.0	C D Holmes 50 nhp 3-cyl 10.0 knots	William R Leyman, Hull

Built by Head & Riley, Hull (Yard No.18). 17.05.1886: Registered at Hull (H1494). 06.06.1893: Re-registered. Lengthened to 103.0
ft by Cochrane's; new engine and boiler fitted; tonnages amended to 159grt, 64net.
14.02.1903: Sold to Charles H Double, Hull. Fishing from Fleetwood. 17.02.1903: Hull registry closed. 18.02.1903: Registered at
Fleetwood (FD204). 03.12.1906: Sold to Ernest Crosby, Fleetwood. 20.12.1906: Sold to John S Doig, Grimsby, & Walter Bacon,
Fleetwood. 05.1910: Sold to A Bannister, Grimsby. 07.05.1910: Fleetwood registry closed. 09.05.1910: Registered at Grimsby
(GY531). 1911: New boiler fitted. 12.1913: Sold to Warberg Exportaffär, Warberg, Sweden. 04.12.1913: Grimsby registry closed.
Renamed **MEERA**. 1920s: Sold to A/B Bergelin & Reuter, Gothenburg. Pre-1927: Sold to Trawl A/B Meera, Gothenburg.
Pre-1930: Sold to Folke Berntsson, Edshultshall, Sweden. 1932: Sold to Fiskeri A/B Hebriderna, Gothenburg.
04.04.1941: Wrecked off Iceland.

M.S. & L. LIGHTER Lighter	89 1893	120		N/A	Manchester, Sheffield & Lincolnshire Railway Co.
M.S. & L. LIGHTER Lighter	90 1893	120		N/A	Manchester, Sheffield & Lincolnshire Railway Co.
M.S. & L. LIGHTER Lighter	91 1893	120		N/A	Manchester, Sheffield & Lincolnshire Railway Co.
RONDO 99707 Iron built steam GY528 trawler	92 01.08.1893 26.08.1893	117 36	87.0 20.0 10.7	C D Holmes 44 nhp 2-cyl 10.0 knots	George F Sleight, Grimsby

26.08.1893: Registered at Grimsby (GY528). 11.1914: Requisitioned for war service as an auxiliary patrol vessel (Ad.No.666).
03.03.1915: Wrecked in the Shetland Isles. No casualties. 25.10.1915: Grimsby registry closed.

IMBRICARIA 99710 Iron built steam GY537 trawler	93 29.08.1893 18.09.1893	150 66	101.0 20.5	C D Holmes 45 nhp 3-cyl 10.0 knots	International Steam Trawling Co Ltd, Grimsby

18.09.1893: Registered at Grimsby (GY537). 1902: Sold to North Eastern Fishing Co Ltd, Grimsby. 1911: New boiler fitted.
06.1912: Sold to British Columbian Fisheries Ltd, London. 19.08.1916: Sold to Canadian Fishing Co Ltd, Vancouver, British
Columbia. 30.09.1916: Grimsby registry closed. Pre-1927: Sold to International Towing Co Ltd, Vancouver.
1927: Sold to Dominion Tug & Barge Co Ltd, Vancouver, and employed as a tug. 1939: Sold to Island Tug & Barge Co Ltd, Victoria,
British Columbia. 1928: Sold to International Towing Co Ltd, Vancouver. 1937: Sold to Goose Island Fisheries Ltd, Goose Island,
British Columbia, and converted to a sailing vessel (ketch). Tonnages amended to 144grt, 144net.
1946: Sold for breaking up.

GERMANIA 99711 Iron built steam GY540 trawler	94 11.09.1893 11.10.1893	150 66	101.0 20.5	C D Holmes 45 nhp 3-cyl 10.0 knots	International Steam Trawling Co Ltd, Grimsby

12.10.1893: Registered at Grimsby (GY540). 07.1898: Sold to North Eastern Fishing Co Ltd, Grimsby.
29.07.1900: Foundered 90 miles east by north of Blyth following a collision with Danish steamer GLÆGERSBORG (1797grt/1883).
08.08.1900: Grimsby registry closed.

TASMANIA 99716 Iron built steam GY554 trawler	95 10.10.1893 06.11.1893	150 66	101.0 20.5 11.0	C D Holmes 45 nhp 3-cyl 10.0 knots	International Steam Trawling Co Ltd, Grimsby

07.11.1893: Registered at Grimsby (GY554). 11.1898: Sold to North Eastern Steam Fishing Co Ltd, Grimsby.
06.1912: Sold to Consolidated Whaling & Deep Sea Fishing Co of South Africa Ltd, London. 11.10.1912: Stranded on rocks near
Danger Point, Dyers Island, Cape Colony, whilst on passage from Grimsby towards Port Natal, South Africa. Crew rescued.
15.11.1912: Grimsby registry closed.

JULES ORBAN DE XIVRY Iron built steam O35 trawler	96 26.10.1893 02.12.1893	148 58	102.0 20.5 11.0	C D Holmes 49 nhp 3-cyl 10.0 knots	Pêcheries Ostendaises, Ostend, Belgium

1902: Sold to Barnard Brieux, Ostend. 1903: Sold to A Golder & B Brieux, Ostend. 11.12.1907: Foundered in rough seas 20 miles
SE of Start Point. Crew saved.

China (97)

(George Scales collection)

The buildings at the far right of this image of the **Danube** (102) have clearly been drawn on at some stage.

(Barnard & Straker collection)

CHINA 99717 Iron built steam GY557 trawler	97 09.11.1893 01.01.1894	170 77	105.5 21.0 11.5	C D Holmes 50 nhp 3-cyl 10.0 knots	International Steam Trawling Co Ltd, Grimsby

02.01.1894: Registered at Grimsby (GY557).   30.06.1898: Sold to North Eastern Steam Fishing Co Ltd, Grimsby.
1900: Lengthened to 115.5ft; tonnages amended to 190grt, 93net.   01.1915: Requisitioned for war service as a minesweeper   (1-6pdr HA) (Ad.No.946).   1919: Returned.   11.1919: North Eastern Steam Fishing Co Ltd in voluntary liquidation.
1919: Sold to Thomas W Baskcomb, Grimsby.   10.1935: Fleet of Thomas W Baskcomb sold to Fred Parkes, Blackpool.
1936: Sold for breaking up.   24.04.1936: Grimsby registry closed.

INDIA 99720 Iron built steam GY570 trawler	98 23.01.1894 10.02.1894	171 77	105.8 21.0 11.5	C D Holmes 50 nhp 3-cyl 10.0 knots	International Steam Trawling Co Ltd, Grimsby

10.02.1894: Registered at Grimsby (GY570).   30.06.1898: Sold to North Eastern Steam Fishing Co Ltd, Grimsby.
1900: Lengthened to 115.5ft; tonnages amended to 190grt, 93net.
11.1919: North Eastern Steam Fishing Co Ltd in voluntary liquidation.   1919: Sold to Thomas W Baskcomb, Grimsby.
10.1935: Fleet of Thomas W Baskcomb sold to Fred Parkes, Blackpool.   1937 Sold for breaking up.
18.03.1937: Grimsby registry closed.

JAMESIA 99718 Iron built steam GY562 trawler	99 01.1894 17.01.1894	171 77	105.5 21.0 11.5	C D Holmes 50 nhp 3-cyl 10.0 knots	North Eastern Steam Fishing Co Ltd, Grimsby

16.01.1894: Registered at Grimsby (GY562).   1900: Lengthened to 115.5ft; tonnages amended to 191grt, 93net.
25.03.1902: Stranded at Bernvik, Iceland.   29.04.1902: Grimsby registry closed - "Wrecked".

KALMIA 104161 Iron built steam GY572 trawler	100 08.02.1894 24.02.1894	171 77	105.7 21.0 11.5	C D Holmes 50 nhp 3-cyl 10.0 knots	North Eastern Steam Fishing Co Ltd, Grimsby

24.02.1894: Registered at Grimsby (GY572).   1900: Lengthened to 115.8ft; tonnages amended to 189grt, 93net.
1912: New boiler fitted.   01.1915: Requisitioned for war service as a minesweeper (1-6pdr HA) (Ad.No.1778).
07.10.1918: Damaged by fire at Stavros in Greece whilst serving with the Royal Navy.
18.02.1919: Grimsby registry closed - "Vessel Lost".
1919: Sold to G Goulandris, Piraeus, Greece, in damaged condition. Repaired and renamed GEORGIOS GOULANDRIS.
1919: Sold to G Pinotsis, Piraeus, and renamed ARTEMISSIA.   1939: Sold to Atid Nav Co Ltd, Haifa, Palestine, and renamed AMOS.
10.1939: Requisitioned for war service as a minesweeper (Mediterranean Command); hire rate £90.0.0d per month.
11.1939: Hire rate reduced to £75.0.0d per month.   12.1939: Returned. Employed as a cargo vessel.
1948: Removed from Lloyd's Register of Shipping.

KATE	101				Vessel contemplated but not built.

DANUBE 102939 Iron built steam H240 trawler	102 10.03.1894 10.04.1894	129 46	92.8 20.5 11.1	C D Holmes 43 nhp 2-cyl 10.0 knots	Thomas Hamling, Hull

10.04.1894: Registered at Hull (H240).   02.03.1898: Sold to T Hamling & Co Ltd, Hull.
02.03.1898: Re-registered. Lengthened to 104.7ft; tonnages amended to 149grt, 63net.
29.12.1905: Sold to M/V Gelderland, IJmuiden, Holland.   29.12.1905: Hull registry closed. Renamed MARIE R OMMERING
(IJM135).   1908: Sold to NV Algemeene Vissch Maats, IJmuiden.   11.1914: New boiler fitted.   1920: Sold to De V E M, IJmuiden.
1926: Sold to C de Vries Czn, IJmuiden; renamed BEGONIA (IJM135).   1926: Sold to NV Vissch Maats 'Begonia', IJmuiden.
1932: Sold to C D Van Vrede, IJmuiden.   1936: Sold to NV Vissch Maats 'Ancor', IJmuiden. Renamed ANCOR (IJM135).
1950: Sold for breaking up.

POTOMAC 102942 Iron built steam H242 trawler	103 05.04.1894 24.04.1894	129 46	92.8 20.5 11.1	C D Holmes 43 nhp 2-cyl 10.0 knots	Thomas Hamling, Hull

20.04.1894: Registered at Hull (H242).   30.11.1897: Re-registered. Lengthened to 104.7ft; tonnages amended to 148grt, 63net.
30.11.1899: Sold to T Hamling & Co Ltd, Hull.   29.12.1905: Sold to M/V Gelderland, IJmuiden, Holland.
29.12.1905: Hull registry closed. Renamed CATHARINA DUYVIS (IJM133).   1908: Sold to NV Algemeene Vissch Maats, IJmuiden.
1920: Sold to De V E M, IJmuiden.   1926: Sold to C de Vries, IJmuiden. Renamed CLYVIA (IJM133).
1926: Sold to NV Vissch Maats 'Clyvia', IJmuiden.   1935: Sold to NV Zee Maats Alaska II, IJmuiden. Renamed SPERWER (IJM133).
08.10.1938: Stranded on north side of Ameland, Holland, having lost propeller. Total loss.

DIAMOND 104168 Iron built steam GY603 trawler	104 07.05.1894 29.05.1894	150 63	101.0 20.5 11.0	C D Holmes 45 nhp 3-cyl 10.0 knots	Thomas C & F Moss, Grimsby

29.05.1894: Registered at Grimsby (GY603).   29.5.1917: Requisitioned for Fishery Reserve (1-6pdr HA). Renamed DIAMOND III.
1919: Released and reverted to DIAMOND (GY603).   01.1946: Sold to Jubilee Fishing Co Ltd, London; continued to fish from
Grimsby.   07.1952: Sold for breaking up. Grimsby registry closed.

MONARCH 104196　Iron built steam GY748　trawler	122 12.02.1895 14.03.1895	130 47	93.6 20.5 11.0	C D Holmes 40 rhp　3-cyl 10.0 knots	Anchor Steam Fishing Co Ltd, Grimsby

13.03.1895: Registered at Grimsby (GY748).　03.1899: Sold to Stephen Williamson, Liverpool (Michael Doig, Aberdeen, manager).
20.03.1899: Grimsby registry closed.　30.03.1899: Registered at Aberdeen (A35).　1906: Sold to Thomas Davidson, Aberdeen.
29.05.1917: Requisitioned for Fishery Reserve. Renamed **MONARCH IV**.　1919: Released and reverted to **MONARCH** (A35).
02.1929: Sold to W Hutchings, Lowestoft.　04.02.1929: Aberdeen registry closed.　06.02.1929: Registered at Lowestoft (LT14).
1937: Sold to G A Breach, Lowestoft.　09.1938: Sold to Belgium for breaking up.　08.10.1938: Lowestoft registry closed.

EMPEROR 104197　Iron built steam GY754　trawler	123 28.02.1895 28.03.1895	130 47	93.6 20.5 11.0	C D Holmes 40 rhp　3-cyl 10.0 knots	Anchor Steam Fishing Co Ltd, Grimsby

23.03.1895: Registered at Grimsby (GY754).　04.1899: Sold to Peter Johnston, Aberdeen.　14.04.1899: Grimsby registry closed.
18.04.1899: Registered at Aberdeen (A39).　1905: Sold to Dublin Steam Trawling Co Ltd, Dublin.
10.1905: Aberdeen registry closed.　Registered at Dublin (D196).　08.1917: Sold to George F Sleight, Grimsby.
08.1917: Dublin registry closed.　18.08.1917: Registered at Grimsby (GY1099).　10.1920: Sold to A Walker, Aberdeen.
25.10.1920: Grimsby registry closed.　17.11.1920: Registered at Aberdeen (A610).　10.02.1926: Foundered 10 miles E by N of
Aberdeen following collision with trawler OCEAN PRINCE (A576) (230grt/1902).　18.02.1926: Aberdeen registry closed.

BARON DE NÈVE DE RODEN 　　　　Iron built steam O754　trawler	124 16.05.1895 28.05.1895	151 71	102.0 20.6 11.0	C D Holmes 51 nhp　3-cyl 10.0 knots	Soc Anon des Pêcheries Ostendaises, Ostend, Belgium

1902: Sold to J Huret, Boulogne, France, and renamed **SIRIUS**.　1904: Sold to Del Rio & Co, Ferrol, Spain.
1920: Sold to Luis Lamigueiro Y Jove, San Sebastián. By 1927: Sold to Pescaderias Coruñesas SA, Madrid.　Registered at San
Sebastián.　15.04.1935: Wrecked approximately 30 miles north of Kenitra, Morocco.

ORONTES 105040　Iron built steam H282　trawler	125 30.03.1895 04.05.1895	178 76	111.4 21.0 11.0	C D Holmes 60 rhp　3-cyl 10.0 knots	Thomas Hamling & Co Ltd, Hull

03.05.1895: Registered at Hull (H282).　28.11.1905: Sold to James A Robertson, Fleetwood.
30.12.1905: Sold to Lancashire Steam Fishing Co Ltd, Fleetwood.　04.01.1906: Hull registry closed.
09.01.1906: Registered at Fleetwood (FD54).　1909: New boiler fitted.　1912: Sold to Wallace Fisheries, Vancouver, British
Columbia.　17.02.1912: Fleetwood registry closed.　Registered at Vancouver, British Columbia.
06.1919: Sold to Northwold Steam Fishing Co Ltd, Grimsby.　7.1919: Vancouver registry closed.
09.07.1919: Registered at Grimsby (GY411).　01.1924: Sold to Robert D Roberts, Grimsby & H P Capron, Cleethorpes.
09.1926: Sold to Orontes Steam Fishing Co Ltd, Grimsby.　01.1933: Sold to A McKay, Milford Haven.
1935: Sold to R L Hancock, Milford Haven.　09.1937: Sold to ship breakers in the Netherlands for breaking up.
08.09.1937: Grimsby registry closed.

BEECHWOLD 105523　Iron built steam GY779　trawler	126 11.05.1895 27.06.1895	129 43	93.5 20.5 11.0	Amos & Smith 35 rhp　3-cyl 9.5 knots	Northwold Steam Fishing Co Ltd, Grimsby

26.06.1895: Registered at Grimsby (GY779).　08.1914: Requisitioned for war service.　09.1914: Returned.
23.09.1916: Stopped by U-boat (UC16) 40 miles SE by E of Spurn Light Vessel and sunk by gunfire (53.12N 01.10E).
All crew saved.　12.10.1916: Grimsby registry closed.

FALCON 105525　Iron built steam GY798　trawler	127 10.07.1895 10.08.1895	154 62	102.7 20.5 11.0	C D Holmes 50 rhp　3-cyl 10.0 knots	Thomas Baskcomb, Grimsby

13.08.1895: Registered at Grimsby (GY798).　01.1903: Sold Sold to Taylor, Olsen, & Pennell, Grimsby.
29.05.1917: Requisitioned for Fishery Reserve.　1919: Released.　11.1923: Sold to Nordzee V/M, IJmuiden, Holland.
28.11.1923: Grimsby registry closed.　Renamed **OLGA** (IJM20).　1925: Sold to W J Kermer, IJmuiden.
1927: Sold to N V Noordzee Exploit Mij, IJmuiden.　1928: Sold to N V Vissch Maats 'Olga', IJmuiden.
1930: Sold to V/M Zuiderhaaks, IJmuiden.　04.04.1936: Sold to shipbreakers in Holland.　1938: Broken up.

URSULA 105526　Iron built steam GY806　trawler	128 26.06.1895 07.09.1895	141 53	93.6 20.4 11.0	Earle's SB & Eng Co Ltd 44 rhp　3-cyl 10.0 knots	Grimsby Union Steam Fishing Co Ltd, Grimsby

05.09.1895: Registered at Grimsby.　05.1906: Sold to Companhia Portuguesa de Pesca, Lisbon, Portugal.
18.05.1906: Grimsby registry closed. Renamed **ALDA BEMVINDA** (B489).　1906: New boiler fitted.
03.1908: Sold to Grampian Fishing Co Ltd, Aberdeen.　12.03.1908: Renamed **CAIRNWELL** (A198).
1911: Sold to William A Leith & William J Duncan, Aberdeen.　1916: Sold to Croston Steam Fishing Co Ltd, Fleetwood.
29.05.1917: Requisitioned for Fishery Reserve.　1919: Released.　03.03.1919: Aberdeen registry closed.
09.03.1919: Registered at Fleetwood (FD45).　23.04.1919: Sold to Cairn Steam Trawling Co Ltd, Liverpool.
01.1920: Sold to Viuda & Sobrinos de Manuel Camara, Spain.　16.01.1920: Fleetwood registry closed. Renamed **PEREZ GALDOS**.
Registered at San Sebastián.　1925: Sold to Ciriza & Cia, San Sebastián.　Renamed **FELISA CIRIZA**.
1930: Sold to Agustin Ciriza, San Sebastián.　1931: Renamed **FELIX CIRIZA**. 1950: Sold to Casa Ciriza S L, San Sebastián.
1977: Sold to Pedro Salas Asensio, San Sebastián.　1981: Removed from Lloyd's Register of Shipping.

UNDAUNTED 105528　Iron built steam GY820　　trawler	129 10.07.1895 18.09.1895	141 53	93.5 20.3 11.0	Earle's SB & Eng Co Ltd 44 rhp　3-cyl 10.0 knots	Grimsby Union Steam Fishing Co Ltd, Grimsby	

20.09.1895: Registered at Grimsby (GY820).　04.1899: Sold to Thomas Davidson, Aberdeen.　17.04.1899: Grimsby registry closed.
15.05.1899: Registered at Aberdeen (A49).　29.05.1917: Requisitioned for Fishery Reserve.　1919: Released.
1925: Sold to Joly & Paumier, Dieppe, France.　26.03.1926: Aberdeen registry closed.　Renamed **ANDRÉ MARCELLE**; tonnages re-measured to 137grt, 38net.　1932: Sold to S A d'Armement Mallet, Dieppe, and renamed **AS-DE-TRÈFLE**.
1952: Sold for breaking up.

RHENO 105524　Iron built steam GY796　　trawler	130 06.1895 06.07.1895	120 34	89.7 20.0 11.0	C D Holmes 40 rhp　3-cyl 10.0 knots	George F Sleight, Grimsby	

08.07.1895: Registered at Grimsby (GY796).　20.10.1908: Foundered following collision with trawler CRUX (GY106) (132grt/1896)
17 miles E by S of the Spurn Light Vessel.　20.10.1908: Grimsby registry closed.

WALES 105055　Iron built steam H289　　trawler	131 24.06.1895 24.07.1895	139 57	98.8 20.5 11.0	Amos & Smith 35 rhp　3-cyl 9.5 knots	Hull Steam Fishing & Ice Co Ltd, Hull	

24.07.1895: Registered at Hull (H289).　06.1914: Sold to W Putz, Geestemünde, Germany.　23.06.1914: Hull registry closed.
Renamed **SÜD** (PG195).　1919: Vessel removed from Lloyd's Register of Shipping.　War loss.

CAMPANIA 105067　Iron built steam H297　　trawler	132 21.09.1895 09.10.1895	167 67	109.0 21.0 11.0	C D Holmes 60 rhp　3-cyl 10.5 knots	Edward J Williams & Co Ltd, Hull	

09.10.1895: Registered at Hull (H297).　27.10.1904: Hull registry closed.　31.10.1904: Sold to Neale & West Ltd, Cardiff. Registered at Cardiff (CF1).　01.1912: Sold to William Walker, Aberdeen.　01.1912: Cardiff registry closed.
13.01.1912: Registered at Aberdeen (A437).　26.06.1915: Stopped by U-boat (U.39) 60 miles N by W of Hoy Head and sunk by gunfire. All crew saved.　05.07.1915: Aberdeen registry closed.

SIR EDWARD WATKIN 　　　Water boat	133 1895	30		N/A		

Recorded on Cochrane's yard list as RHINO.

NEWFOUNDLAND 105059　Iron built steam H292　　trawler	134 08.08.1895 03.09.1895	139 58	98.5 20.5 11.0	Amos & Smith 35 rhp　3-cyl 9.5 knots	Hull Steam Fishing & Ice Co Ltd, Hull	

03.09.1895: Registered at Hull (H292).　15.02.1898: Sailed from Hull for North Sea grounds. Later posted missing. No survivors.
04.03.1898: Hull registry closed.

ONTARIO 105064　Iron built steam H294　　trawler	135 26.08.1895 25.09.1895	139 58	98.5 20.5 11.0	Amos & Smith 35 rhp　3-cyl 9.5 knots	Hull Steam Fishing & Ice Co Ltd, Hull	

26.09.1895: Registered at Hull (H294).　06.1914: Sold to V Putz & Co, Geestemünde, Germany.
23.06.1914: Hull registry closed.　Renamed **WEST** (PG197).　07.10.1915: Captured by HMS MANLY in North Sea.
10.1915: Renamed **CUDWOSIN** (Ad.No.1944). Commissioned as a minesweeper (1-6pdr).　1917: New boiler fitted.
16.03.1920: Sold by auction at Aberdeen to Thomas T Brown & George Brown, Leith, for £2300.
03.07.1920: Renamed **SETON CASTLE** (GN65).　06.1924: Sold to Edward J Hellings, Milford Haven, & Hans B Tyvold, Hakin.
28.06.1924: Granton registry closed.　03.07.1924: Registered at Milford (M27).　06.04.1926: Towed disabled Glasgow steam coaster OLIVINE (754grt/1918) to Holyhead.　Pre 1927: Sold to Edward J Hellings, Milford Haven.
23.12.1932: Sold to Ernest C A Clarke, London.　02.1933: Sold to Jaques A Testulat, Dieppe, France.
28.02.1933: Milford registry closed.　02.1933: Renamed **ABYSSINIA**.　22.08.1933: Foundered near Portsail, Finisterre.

BERMUDA 105066　Iron built steam H296　　trawler	136 05.09.1895 09.10.1895	139 58	98.4 20.4 11.0	Amos & Smith 35 rhp　3-cyl 9.5 knots	Hull Steam Fishing & Ice Co Ltd, Hull	

09.10.1895: Registered at Hull (H296).　15.02.1900: Sailed Hull for North Sea grounds. Later posted missing. No survivors.
23.04.1900: Hull registry closed.

VANCOUVER 105070　Iron built steam H299　　trawler	137 07.09.1895 24.10.1895	139 58	98.4 20.4 11.0	Amos & Smith 35 rhp　3-cyl 9.5 knots	Hull Steam Fishing & Ice Co Ltd, Hull	

24.10.1895: Registered at Hull (H299).　06.1914: Sold to V Putz & Co, Geestemünde, Germany.　23.06.1914: Hull registry closed.
Renamed **NORD** (PG194).　1919: Vessel removed from Lloyd's Register of Shipping. War loss.

TOURQUENNOIS O125	Iron built steam trawler	191 14.07.1897 05.03.1898	170 69	110.7 21.0 11.0	C D Holmes 64 rhp 3-cyl	H Aspeslagh & F Zonnekyn, Ostend

3.1898: Registered at Ostend (O125).   01.08.1909: Foundered following collision 6 miles NE of Pendeen Watch Lighthouse, Cornwall.   Ostend registry closed.

ATLANTIC 109021 H392	Iron built steam trawler	192 24.02.1898 20.04.1898	176 57	110.0 21.0 11.3	C D Holmes 58 rhp 3-cyl 10.0 knots	William C Edwards & Co Ltd Hull

22.04.1898: Registered at Hull (H392).   24.03.1900: Sold to Daniel J McKinnon Snr, Dundee.   24.03.1900: Hull registry closed.
03.1900: Registered at Dundee (DE126).   29.05.1917: Requisitioned for Fishery Reserve.   1919: Released.
07.1917: Sold to W Crampin, Grimsby.   07.1917: Dundee registry closed.   23.07.1917: Registered at Grimsby (GY1085).
11.1919: Sold to W Jagger, Grimsby.   04.1920: Sold to Headway Steam Fishing Co Ltd, Grimsby.
04.1923: Sold to W Allen, Grimsby.   01.1927: Sold to William Lambert, Cleethorpes.   05.1930: Sold to J Doig, Grimsby.
07.1930: Sold to John Chant, Plymouth.   1931: Sold to Plymouth Trawlers Ltd, Plymouth.   1939: Sold to Percy V Turner, Plymouth.
06.1954: Sank alongside in Sutton Harbour, Plymouth, refloated and sold to Demmelweek & Redding Ltd, Plymouth, for breaking up.

BUZZARD 109814 GY825	Iron built steam trawler	193 21.07.1898 01.09.1898	181 65	109.1 21.0 11.3	C D Holmes 50 rhp 3-cyl 10.0 knots	Thomas Baskcomb, Grimsby

05.09.1898: Registered at Grimsby (GY825).   01.1911: Sold to Alick Black, Grimsby.   12.1912: Sold to A Bannister, Cleethorpes.
02.1916: Sold to East Anglian Steam Fishing Co Ltd, Grimsby.   29.05.1917: Requisitioned for Fishery Reserve.
Renamed **BUZZARD II**.   1919: Released and reverted to **BUZZARD** (GY825).   01.1920: Sold to A Bannister, Grimsby.
1928: New boiler fitted.   11.1931: Sold to T Ross, Grimsby.   05.1932: Sold to B H Bannister, Grimsby.
1939: Transferred to Executors of late B H Bannister, Grimsby, but not sold on after probate.
09.06.1940: Requisitioned for war service on Examining Service. Renamed **ARREST**; hire rate £45.5.0d per month.
06.1940: Fitted for boom defence duties (P. No. Z246).   07.1945: Returned and reverted to **BUZZARD** (GY825).   1948: Laid up.
1949: Sold to BISCO and allocated to Clayton & Davie Ltd, Dunston-on-Tyne, for breaking up.   07.1949: Arrived River Tyne.
Grimsby registry closed.

GOLDFINDER 108500 GY526	Iron built steam trawler	194 25.02.1898	162 64	100.0 20.6 11.0	Amos & Smith 45 rhp 3-cyl 10.0 knots	Ernest Michael Willey North, Grimsby

26.02.1898: Registered at Grimsby (GY526).   21.02.1900: Sold to Peter Llewellyn Hancock, Milford Haven.
17.04.1901: Sold to John William Wilkins under mortgage.   20.09.1903: Sold to Miss Florrie Wilkin, Milford Haven.
08.04.1904: Sold to John Setterfield, Milford Haven.   20.03.1908: Foundered 12 miles north of Godrevy Island, St. Ives, Cornwall, after beam trawl iron damaged shell plates. The eight crew (Skipper John Setterfield) took to boat and picked up by Brixham sailing trawler SUPREME (BM97) (Skipper J E Babb) which had been fishing nearby. Landed at St Ives.
30.03.1908: Grimsby registry closed.

PINEWOLD 109523 GY609	Iron built steam trawler	195 1898 07.04.1898	147 41	96.7 19.9 11.2	Amos & Smith 36 rhp 3-cyl 10.0 knots	Northwold Steam Fishing Co Ltd, Grimsby

14.04.1898: Registered at Grimsby (GY609).   11.1904: Sold to Norway.   01.11.1904: Grimsby registry closed.
08.1906: Sold to Northwold Fishing Co Ltd, Grimsby.   31.08.1906: Registered at Grimsby (GY177).   1912: New boiler fitted.
29.05.1917: Requisitioned for Fishery Reserve.   1919: Released.   06.1922: Sold to Cockerill & Co, Milford Haven.
11.1922: Sold to Wattez Frères, Boulogne, France.   29.11.1922: Grimsby registry closed. Renamed **JEAN LOUISE**.
1932: Sold to Ch Gueulle Fils, Boulogne. Renamed **MARIE JEANNINE**.   09.1952: Sold for breaking up.

PÊCHERIES OSTENDAISES IV O65	Iron built steam trawler	196 1897 07.04.1898	159 61	102.0 20.5 11.2	C D Holmes 52 rhp 3-cyl	Soc Anon des Pêcheries Ostendaises, Ostend, Belgium

04.1898: Registered at Ostend (O65).   1906: Sold to Alfred T Golder & Co, Ostend.
12.07.1910: Foundered after striking sunken wreckage 28 miles west-south-west of Beachy Head. Crew saved. Ostend registry closed.

PÊCHERIES OSTENDAISES V		197				Vessel contemplated but not built.

CHESHIRE 109546 GY742	Iron built steam trawler	198 09.05.1898 09.06.1898	148 51	97.3 20.5 11.0	C D Holmes 40 rhp 3-cyl 10.0 knots	North Lincolnshire Steam Fishing Co Ltd, Grimsby

16.06.1898: Registered at Grimsby (GY742).   07.07.1915: Mined, 50 miles E by N of Spurn Point. Eight crew lost.
15.7.1915: Grimsby registry closed.

DEVONSHIRE 109802 GY766	Iron built steam trawler	199 09.05.1898 22.06.1898	148 51	97.3 20.5 11.0	C D Holmes 40 rhp 3-cyl 10.0 knots	North Lincolnshire Steam Fishing Co Ltd, Grimsby

23.06.1898: Registered at Grimsby (GY766).   24.09.1916: Stopped by U-boat (U57) 33 miles NE1/2N of the Spurn Light Vessel, and sunk. All crew survived.   12.10.1916: Grimsby registry closed.

KELVIN 109040 Iron built steam H405 trawler	200 22.02.1898 15.07.1898	188 62	112.0 21.0 11.3	C D Holmes 60 rhp 3-cyl	F & T Ross Ltd, Hull

18.07.1898: Registered at Hull (H405).   05.03.1907: Sold to William R Cruckshank, Glasgow.
03.1907: Sold to Alfonso R del Valle, Aviles, Spain.   11.03.1907: Hull registry closed.
1914: Sold to Fernandez Seferino, Barcelona.   1915: Sold to Italian Government and renamed **MARIE LOUISE**.
1916: Vessel removed from Lloyd's Register of Shipping; possible war loss.

LA CANACHE Iron built steam B2542 trawler	201 27.10.1897 10.05.1898	153 18	97.0 20.6 11.0	Amos & Smith 36 nhp 3-cyl	Vidor Frères et Cie, Boulogne, France

1908: Sold to Lucien Calamel, Le Tréport, France (DI439).   1923: Sold to Pêcheries et Glacières Du, Le Tréport .
1936: Sold to Lucien Calamel, Le Tréport.   1938: Sold for breaking up.

EBRO 109547 Iron built steam GY743 trawler	202 23.04.1898 16.06.1898	175 60	100.2 21.0 11.6	Amos & Smith 45 rhp 3-cyl 10.0 knots	Ocean Steam Fishing Co Ltd, Grimsby

17.06.1898: Registered at Grimsby (GY743).   12.1914: Requisitioned for war service (1-3pdr) (Ad.No.998).
06.1915: Renamed **EBRO II**.   1921: Returned and reverted to **EBRO** (GY743).   22.04.1919: Sold to F Bacon, Grimsby.
06.1919: Sold to Economy Steam Fishing Co Ltd, Grimsby.   03.1920: Sold to H Bacon, Grimsby.
03.1920: Sold to Trawlers White Sea & Grimsby Ltd, Grimsby.   04.1921: Sold to Lord High Admiral's Office, London.
06.1921: Sold to Cailliez et Lézier, Boulogne, France.   21.06.1921: Grimsby registry closed.   Registered at Boulogne.
Re-measured 183grt, 53net.   1928: Sold to Quillon & Capion, Dieppe.   1929: Sold to G Jacquemard, Dieppe.
1932: Sold to Neveu et Boudet, Dieppe.   1950: Sold to Mougin, Fils, Dieppe, and renamed **ARACK**.
1960: Vessel removed from Lloyd's Register of Shipping.

FERMO 109805 Iron built steam GY773 trawler	203 23.05.1898 09.07.1898	175 60	100.1 21.0 11.6	Amos & Smith 45 rhp 3-cyl 10.0 knots	Ocean Steam Fishing Co Ltd, Grimsby

12.07.1898: Registered at Grimsby (GY773).   1917: Requisitioned for Fishery Reserve.
10.11.1917: Foundered 3 miles NE of the Humber Light Vessel following collision with the Norwegian steamer
BREIDABLIK (1116grt/1910).   19.11.1917: Grimsby registry closed.

CAPTAIN 109006 Iron built steam H382 trawler	204 12.10.1897 24.11.1897	188 66	112.6 21.0 11.6	Bailey & Leetham 50 rhp 3-cyl 10.0 knots	East Coast Steam Trawling Co Ltd, Hull

23.11.1897: Registered at Hull (H382).   12.03.1901: Sold to John Hawkins Luxton & William Kent, Plymouth.
29.05.1901: Vessel foundered off Ile d'Ushant, France.   13.06.1901: Hull registry closed.

VALERIA 109813 Iron built steam GY818 trawler	205 1898 20.08.1898	189 66	112.6 21.0 11.6	C D Holmes 55 rhp 3-cyl	Arctic Steam Fishing Co Ltd, Grimsby

23.08.1898: Registered at Grimsby (GY818).   18.08.1916: Sold to Consolidated Steam Fishing & Ice Co Ltd, Grimsby.
29.05.1917: Requisitioned for Fishery Reserve.   1919: Released.   01.04.1924: Transferred to Lowestoft.
08.01.1925: Grimsby registry closed.   09.01.1925: Registered at Lowestoft (LT156).   09.1927: Owners re-styled Consolidated
Fisheries Ltd, Grimsby.   18.08.1940: Foundered 8 miles from the Smalls Light Vessel following enemy air attack. All crew saved.
12.09.1940: Lowestoft registry closed.

VICEROY 109808 Iron built steam GY786 liner	206 09.06.1898 27.07.1898	217 94	114.0 21.0 11.6	Amos & Smith 50 rhp 3-cyl	Atlas Steam Fishing Co Ltd, Grimsby

29.07.1898: Registered at Grimsby (GY786).   07.12.1915: Posted missing on a North Sea trip. No survivors.
21.01.1916: Grimsby registry closed - "Vessel missing".

CASSOWARY 109527 Iron built steam GY634 liner	207 24.03.1898 02.05.1898	203 76	114.0 21.0 11.5	C D Holmes 60 rhp 3-cyl	Thomas Baskcomb, Grimsby

03.05.1898: Registered at Grimsby (GY634).   03.1909: Lengthened by W H Warren, New Holland, to 122.4ft; tonnages amended to
220grt and 89net. New deck fitted. New boiler by Blair & Co Ltd, Stockton-on-Tees.   30.04.1909: Re-registered as a trawler.
23.04.1914: Sold to Mary A Baskcomb, Thomas W Baskcomb, John C Store & Herbert Crabtree, Grimsby.
11.1914: Requisitioned for war service as a minesweeper (1-6pdr) (Ad.No.806).
19.10.1915: Sold to Thomas Baskcomb Ltd, Grimsby.   1919: Returned.
12.07.1933: Company re-styled Amalgamated Steam Fishing Co Ltd, Grimsby.
23.02.1935: Sold to Harry A Baskcomb, Grimsby.   12.1935: Sold for breaking up.   07.12.1935: Grimsby registry closed.

EGRET	208	206	115.7	C D Holmes	Thomas Baskcomb,
110864 Iron built steam	17.01.1899	84	21.0	60 rhp 3-cyl	Grimsby
GY1084 liner/trawler	21.02.1899		11.6		

22.02.1899: Registered at Grimsby (GY1084).   16.06.1908: Lengthened by Charlton & Doughty Ltd, Grimsby, to 123.0ft and part new deck fitted; tonnages amended to 224grt and 91net.
23.04.1914: Transferred to Mary A Baskcomb, Thomas W Baskcomb, John C Store & Herbert Crabtree, Grimsby.
1915: New boiler fitted.   19.10.1915: Sold to Thomas Baskcomb Ltd, Grimsby.   29.05.1917: Requisitioned for Fishery Reserve.
1919: Released.   12.07.1933: Company re-styled Amalgamated Steam Fishing Co Ltd, Grimsby.
23.02.1935: Sold to Harry A Baskcomb, Grimsby.   12.1935: Sold for breaking up.   07.12.1935: Grimsby registry closed.

ADMIRAL	209	188	112.6	Bailey & Leetham	East Coast Steam Trawling
106775 Iron built steam	29.09.1897	66	21.0	50 rhp 3-cyl	Co Ltd,
H376 trawler	21.10.1897		11.6	10.0 knots	Hull

19.10.1897: Registered at Hull (H376).   20.04.1900: Sold to West Riding Steam Fishing Co Ltd, Grimsby.
26.04.1900: Hull registry closed.   27.04.1900: Registered at Grimsby (GY1168).   06.1910: Sold to R W Lewis, Aberdeen.
22.06.1910: Grimsby registry closed.   23.06.1910: Registered at Aberdeen (A315).
10.1911: Sold to Kobe Sanbashi Kabushiki Kaisha, Kobe, Japan, and renamed **DAIGO MARU**.
19.10.1911: Aberdeen registry closed.   1920: Sold to Harashin-Ichi, Nishinomiya.
27.07.1924: Foundered off Notoro following a collision whilst on passage from Otomaru towards Otura.

BANGKOK	210	188	112.6	Bailey & Leetham	East Coast Steam Trawling
106779 Iron built steam	29.09.1897	66	21.0	50 rhp 3-cyl	Co Ltd,
H379 trawler	06.11.1897		11.6	10.0 knots	Hull

04.11.1897: Registered at Hull (H379).   18.05.1900: Sold to West Riding Steam Fishing Co Ltd, Grimsby.
22.05.1900: Hull registry closed.   23.06.1900: Registered at Grimsby (GY1175).
12.1901: Sold to Göteborgs Angefiske Aktieb, Gothenburg, Sweden.   03.12.1901: Grimsby registry closed.
1905: New boiler fitted.   1914: Sold to Fiskeriaktieb Avance, Gothenburg, and renamed **HELGA**.
1926: Sold to Trålaktiebal Falken, Gothenburg.   1929: Sold to NV Stoomvisscherij "Ymond I", IJmuiden, Netherlands (IJM96).
1930: Sold to NV Stoomvisscherij "Emergo", IJmuiden, and renamed **STORMVOGEL** (IJM96).
1931: Sold to NV Visscherij Maats "Ijmond", IJmuiden.   1934: Sold to W Kramer Snr & J P Booij, IJmuiden, and renamed **VIOS IV** (IJM96).   11.11.1941: Bombed and sunk in the North Sea by enemy aircraft.

Egret (208)

(Jonathan Grobler collection)

*Another view of the **Egret**
(Jonathan Grobler collection)*

Cochrane & Cooper Ltd, Beverley

FEDERAL 109017 Iron built steam H390 trawler	211 25.01.1898 29.03.1898	189 67	112.5 21.0 11.6	Bailey & Leetham 50 rhp 3-cyl 10.0 knots	East Coast Steam Trawling Co Ltd, Hull
	30.03.1898: Registered at Hull (H390). 01.1899: Sold to Pelham Steam Fishing Co Ltd, Grimsby. 24.01.1899: Hull registry closed. 24.01.1899: Registered at Grimsby (GY1054). 05.1905: Sold to Neale & West Ltd, Cardiff. 02.05.1905: Grimsby registry closed. 05.1905: Registered at Cardiff (CF17). 1911: Sold to Shinichi Hara, Nagasaki, Japan; renamed **SHINKO MARU No. 1**. 17.04.1914: Foundered following a collision approximately 26 miles south-west of Iwojima.
DERWENT 109014 Iron built steam H387 trawler	212 10.01.1898 08.03.1898	189 67	112.5 21.0 11.6	Bailey & Leetham 50 rhp 3-cyl 10.0 knots	East Coast Steam Trawling Co Ltd, Hull
	28.02.1898: Registered at Hull (H387). 26.10.1899: Sold to Northwold Steam Fishing Co Ltd, Grimsby. 26.10.1899: Hull registry closed. 31.10.1899: Renamed **LIMEWOLD** (GY1125). 12.1914: Requisitioned for war service as a minesweeper (1-6pdr) (Ad.No.771). 1919: Returned. 11.1924: Sold for breaking up. 27.11.1924: Grimsby registry closed.
WINDSOR 109829 Iron built steam GY967 trawler	213 21.09.1898 22.10.1898	172 62	100.0 21.0 11.0	C D Holmes 50 rhp 3-cyl 10.0 knots	Queen Steam Fishing Co Ltd, Grimsby
	24.10.1898: Registered at Grimsby (GY967). 22.01.1915: Mined 55 miles E of Spurn Point. 26.01.1915: Grimsby registry closed.
BALMORAL 109830 Iron built steam GY968 trawler	214 01.10.1898 11.11.1898	172 62	100.0 21.0 11.0	C D Holmes 50 rhp 3-cyl 10.0 knots	Queen Steam Fishing Co Ltd, Grimsby
	12.11.1898: Registered at Grimsby (GY968). 22.01.1915: Posted missing on a North Sea trip. No survivors. 22.03.1915: Grimsby registry closed.
LA VAGUE Iron built steam B2535 trawler	215 10.01.1898 18.03.1898	174 37	100.0 21.5 11.0	Hawthorns & Co 41 nhp 3-cyl 10.0 knots	Delpierre-Noel, Boulogne, France
	1908: Sold to Pêcheries Françaises D'Arcachon Soc Anon, Arcachon, France (ARC8716). 1911: Sold to Micke-Battez, Boulogne. 1910: Sold to Nouvelles Pêcheries Françaises D'Arcachon Soc Anon, Arcachon. 08.06.1915: Wrecked at Soapy Cove, W of The Lizard, Cornwall.

Balmoral (214) being coaled at Grimsby.

(Jonathan Grobler collection)

KESTREL	216	181	109.1	C D Holmes	Thomas Baskcomb,
109817 Iron built steam	21.07.1898	65	21.0	50 rhp 3-cyl	Grimsby
GY831 trawler	12.09.1898		11.3	10.0 knots	

13.09.1898: Registered at Grimsby (GY831).   01.1911: Sold to Alick Black, Grimsby.   12.1912: Sold to A Bannister, Grimsby.
17.03.1917: Stopped and then sunk by U-boat (UC50) 20 miles E by S of Longstone Light. Crew saved.
22.03.1917: Grimsby registry closed.

ANSON	217	172	100.0	C D Holmes	William Grant,
109835 Iron built steam	20.10.1898	62	21.0	50 rhp 3-cyl	Grimsby
GY976 trawler	02.12.1898		11.0	10.0 knots	

02.12.1898: Registered at Grimsby (GY976).   05.06.1904: Foundered 83 miles E by S of Spurn Point following collision with the Danish steamer LONDON (1562grt/1890).   11.06.1904: Grimsby registry closed.

ANLABY	218	191	115.4	C D Holmes	James Henry Collinson,
109091 Iron built steam	20.10.1898	69	21.0	63 rhp 3-cyl	Hull
H437 trawler	13.12.1898		11.5	10.5 knots	

14.12.1898: Registered at Hull (H437).   14.01.1902: Foundered in Grindavik Bay, Iceland.   22.01.1902: Hull registry closed.

ARCTIC	219	187	112.0	Amos & Smith	William C Edwards,
109076 Iron built steam	20.09.1898	66	21.0	50 rhp 3-cyl	Hull
H426 trawler	24.10.1898		11.6	10.0 knots	

25.10.1898: Registered at Hull (H426).   26.03.1900: Sold to Dodds Steam Fishing Co Ltd, North Shields.
26.03.1900: Hull registry closed.   29.03.1900: Registered at North Shields (SN86).
1907: Sold to Empreza Portuense De Pescarias Ld, Oporto, Portugal.   14.04.1907: North Shields registry closed.
Renamed **PORTUENSE**. Registered at Oporto.   12.1911: Stranded. No details given in Lloyd's Casualty Returns.

SYLVIA	220	213	117.6	C D Holmes	Armitage's Steam Trawling
109094 Iron built steam	03.11.1898	73	21.5	60 rhp 3-cyl	Co Ltd,
H439 trawler	21.12.1898		11.5	10.0 knots	Hull

24.12.1898: Registered at Hull (H439).   1914: Transferred to Fleetwood.
06.1915: Requisitioned for war service as a boom defence trawler.   26.01.1918: Sold to Joseph R E Mordaunt, Grimsby.
26.01.1918: Hull registry closed.   30.01.1918: Registered at Grimsby (GY1112).   08.1918: Returned.
10.1918: Sold to H Rackhind, Grimsby.   09.1919: Sold to Faroe Steam Fishing Co Ltd, Grimsby.
11.1921: Sold to Forward Steam Fishing Co Ltd, Grimsby.
07.04.1941: Foundered off Faroe Isles in approximate position 61° 27'N, 05° 48'W after being bombed and damaged by German aircraft. Ten crew rescued, one man lost.   22.07.1941: Grimsby registry closed.

GENERAL	221	191	112.7	Bailey & Leetham	East Coast Steam Trawling
109031 Iron built steam	06.04.1898	70	21.0	50 rhp 3-cyl	Co Ltd,
H397 trawler	01.06.1898		11.6	10.5 knots	Hull

26.05.1898: Registered at Hull (H397).   30.12.1898: Sold to Palatine Steam Fishing Co Ltd, Grimsby.
27.12.1898: Registered at Grimsby (GY1014).   30.12.1898: Hull registry closed.   11.1906: Sold to H B & G W Jeffs, Grimsby.
1914: Sold to Charles Kendall & Co, Aberdeen.   06.11.1914: Grimsby registry closed.   10.11.1914: Registered at Aberdeen (A173).
1915: Sold to Aberdeen General Steam Fishing Co Ltd, Aberdeen.   29.05.1917: Requisitioned for Fishery Reserve.
1918: Sold to Hesketh Steam Trawlers Ltd, Fleetwood.   1919: Released.   07.03.1919: Aberdeen registry closed.
08.03.1919: Registered at Fleetwood (FD76).   1924: Sold to William Grey, Dunbar.
1926: Sold to James Flockhart, Newhaven, Edinburgh.   1927: Sold to NV Visscherij Maats Poolzee, IJmuiden, Holland.
29.11.1927: Fleetwood registry closed.   12.1927: Renamed **POOLZEE** (IJM77).   04.1951: Sold for breaking up.

HALCYON	222	190	112.6	Bailey & Leetham	East Coast Steam Trawling
109044 Iron built steam	08.06.1898	64	21.0	50 rhp 3-cyl	Co Ltd,
H408 trawler	06.08.1898		11.5	10.5 knots	Hull

08.08.1898: Registered at Hull (H408).   25.10.1899: Sold to Cleethorpes Steam Trawling Co Ltd, Grimsby.
03.11.1899: Hull registry closed.   06.11.1899: Registered at Grimsby (GY1126).
01.1916: Sold to H Bacon & H G Hopwood, Grimsby.   01.08.1916: Sold to James Leyman Jnr, Hull.
19.02.1917: Mined whilst fishing near Butt of Lewis, Hebrides. Skipper and nine crewmen lost.
22.02.1917: Grimsby registry closed - "Transferred to Hull".   23.02.1917: Registered at Hull (H535).
23.07.1917: Hull registry closed - "Missing".

IVANHOE	223	190	112.3	Bailey & Leetham	United Steam Fishing
109823 Iron built steam	06.08.1898	67	21.0	50 rhp 3-cyl	Co Ltd,
GY902 trawler	27.09.1898		11.6	10.5 knots	Grimsby

04.11.1898: Registered at Grimsby (GY902).   10.1914: Requisitioned for war service as an auxiliary patrol vessel (Ad.No.664).
03.11.1914: Stranded on Black Rocks, Firth of Forth. All crew saved.   13.07.1915: Grimsby registry closed.

Edison (225)

Merlin (227)

ROWENA 109825 Iron built steam GY915 trawler	224 20.08.1898 08.11.1898	190 67	112.3 21.0 11.6	Bailey & Leetham 50 rhp 3-cyl 10.5 knots	United Steam Fishing Co Ltd, Grimsby

09.11.1898: Registered at Grimsby (GY915).   04.12.1907: Vessel left Grimsby for a North Sea trip. Posted missing. No survivors.
10.01.1908: Grimsby registry closed.

EDISON 109081 Iron built steam H430 trawler	225 17.09.1898 10.11.1898	196 53	115.3 21.0 11.6	Amos & Smith 60 rhp 3-cyl 10.5 knots	F & T Ross Ltd, Hull

12.11.1898: Registered at Hull (H430).   12.1914: Requisitioned for war service as a minesweeper (Ad.No. 395).
06.07.1915: Stranded on Isle of Lewis, Hebrides. Total loss.   10.11.1915: Hull registry closed.

BENBOW 109846 Iron built steam GY1016 trawler	226 17.12.1898 19.01.1899	172 62	100.2 21.0 11.0	C D Holmes 50 rhp 3-cyl 10.0 knots	William Grant, Grimsby

21.01.1899: Registered at Grimsby (GY1016).   09.02.1917: Stopped by U-boat (UB22) 25 miles E by S of Bell Rock and scuttled.
All crew saved.   06.03.1917: Grimsby registry closed.

Cochrane & Cooper Ltd, Beverley (B) & Selby (S) *

MERLIN 110899 Iron built steam GY190 trawler	227 (S) 19.05.1899 22.06.1899	185 60	110.0 21.2 11.2	C D Holmes 50 rhp 3-cyl 10.0 knots	Thomas Baskcomb, Grimsby

23.06.1899: Registered at Grimsby (GY190).   01.1911: Sold to South Western Steam Fishing Co Ltd, Grimsby & Fleetwood.
10.1912: New boiler fitted.   12.1912: Sold to Thomas W Baskcomb, Grimsby.
05.1915: Requisitioned for war service as a minesweeper (1-3pdr) (Ad.No.1794).
03.1916: Sold to Earl Steam Fishing Co Ltd, Grimsby.   08.1916: Sold to H Croft Baker, Grimsby.   1920: Returned.
01.1923: Sold to Savoy Steam Fishing Co Ltd, Cleethorpes.   10.1924: Sold to Henry P Capron, Grimsby.
09.1926: Sold to Orontes Steam Fishing Co Ltd, Grimsby.   11.1932: Sold to Filey United Steam Fishing Co Ltd, Scarborough.
03.1937: Sold for breaking up.   25.03.1937: Grimsby registry closed.

NANDU 110901 Iron built steam GY439 trawler	228 (S) 27.05.1899 05.08.1899	186 68	110.0 21.2 11.2	C D Holmes 50 rhp 3-cyl 10.0 knots	Thomas Baskcomb, Grimsby

07.08.1899: Registered at Grimsby (GY439).   01.1911: Sold to South Western Steam Fishing Co Ltd, Grimsby & Fleetwood.
27.03.1911: Stranded near Skaji, Iceland. Total loss.   24.04.1911: Grimsby registry closed.

AGAMI 110886 Iron built steam GY143 trawler	229 (S) 29.04.1899 03.06.1899	186 63	110.0 21.2 11.2	C D Holmes 50 rhp 3-cyl 10.0 knots	Thomas W Baskcomb, Grimsby

05.06.1899: Registered at Grimsby (GY143).   01.1911: Sold to Marshall Line Steam Fishing Co Ltd, Grimsby.
06.1914: Sold to Savoy Steam Fishing Co Ltd, Grimsby.   11.1915: Sold to J L Green, Grimsby.
29.05.1917: Requisitioned for Fishery Reserve.   1919: Released.
11.1924: Sold to Grimsby Trawler Owners' Direct Fish Supply Co Ltd, Grimsby.   09.1937: Sold for breaking up.
23.09.1937: Grimsby registry closed.

NORSEMAN 110862 Iron built steam GY1072 trawler	230 (B) 26.11.1898 04.02.1899	182 64	110.0 21.2 11.2	Bailey & Leetham 50 rhp 3-cyl 10.0 knots	Metropolitan Steam Fishing Co Ltd, Grimsby

06.02.1899: Registered at Grimsby (GY1072).   31.05.1901: Grimsby registry closed.
05.1901: Sold to Ole Gogstad, Sandefjord, Norway (TG4).   05.1901: Transferred to Sandefjord, Norway.
1908: Sold to Acties Norseman, Sandefjord (SD4).   08.07.1914: Vessel sank following a collision in the North Sea.

BUCKINGHAM 110867 Iron built steam GY1096 trawler	231 (B) 31.01.1899 07.02.1899	172 62	100.0 21.0 11.0	C D Holmes 50 rhp 3-cyl 10.0 knots	Queen Steam Fishing Co Ltd, Grimsby

08.03.1899: Registered at Grimsby (GY1096).   29.05.1917: Requisitioned for Fishery Reserve.   1919: Released.
03.1930: Sold to A Grant & Son Ltd, Grimsby.   08.1930: Renamed **WARREN** (GY1096).
10.1940: Sold to Shire Trawlers Ltd, London.   12.1940: Sold to J Bennett (Wholesale) Ltd, London.
12.1943: Sold to Wembley Steam Fishing Co Ltd, Grimsby.   11.1945: Sold to Samuel Stewart & Co (London) Ltd, London.
01.1946: Grimsby registry closed.   11.01.1946: Registered at Lowestoft (LT117).
25.06.1946: Sold to Cranley Shipping Co Ltd, London.   12.05.1949: Sold to Cranbrook Shipping Co Ltd, London.
04.12.1952: Sold to BISCO and allocated to Tyne-based shipbreakers.   16.04.1952: Sailed Lowestoft for River Tyne.
16.01.1953: Lowestoft registry closed.

* (S) denotes vessel completed at Selby and (B) denotes vessel completed at Beverley. NB - this is for identification in the pages of this book only; the letters were NOT a suffix to the official yard numbers.

Agami (229)

(Authors' collection)

King Erik (233)

(Jonathan Grobler collection)

REGINALD	259 (S)	191	110.7	C D Holmes	Peter L Hancock &
112453 Iron built	10.08.1899	75	21.0	55 rhp 3-cyl	David Pettit,
M149 steam trawler	25.11.1899		11.2	10.0 knots	Hakin

28.11.1899: Registered at Milford (M149). 10.1901: Sold to J H Luxton & William Kent, Plymouth.
28.10.1901: Milford registry closed. 10.1901: Registered at Plymouth (PH75). 1906: In dense fog stranded on south east coast of
St Mary's, Isles of Scilly. Refloated with minor damage. 12.1909: Sold to David Pettit, Milford, & Joseph W Johnston, Llanstadwell.
12.1909: Plymouth registry closed. 14.12.1909: Registered at Milford (M46). 12.02.1910: Renamed **CORNET** (M46).
04.05.1911: Sold to David Pettit, Milford. 30.04.1914: Sold to Edith Kendall & Henry D Fain, Grimsby.
23.08.1915: Sold to Thomas G Hancock, Hakin, & John D Harries, Milford. 12.1916: Sold to Sir George F Sleight, Grimsby.
15.12.1916: Milford registry closed. 19.12.1916: Registered at Grimsby (GY1006). 29.05.1917: Requisitioned for Fishery Reserve.
1919: Released. 10.1920: Sold to Andrew Walker, Aberdeen. 25.10.1920: Grimsby registry closed.
17.11.1920: Registered at Aberdeen (A595). 01.1928: Sold to James Leyman, Hull. 12.01.1928: Aberdeen registry closed.
13.01.1928: Registered at Hull (H377). 07.1929: Sold to Gourney Deplanque & R Nicolas, Boulogne.
23.07.1929: Hull registry closed. 07.1929: Renamed **NICOLAS PIERRE**.
07.10.1931: Foundered following collision near Haaks Light Vessel.

ASSYRIAN	260 (B)	176	110.6	Great Central Co-op	Great Central Co-op
110913 Iron built	10.08.1899	54	21.0	46 rhp 3-cyl	Engineering & Ship Repair
GY877 steam trawler	05.10.1899		11.2	10.0 knots	Co Ltd, Grimsby

03.10.1899: Registered at Grimsby (GY877). 06.1900: Sold to Trempi & Cie, Boulogne, France.
15.06.1900: Grimsby registry closed. 06.1900: Renamed **EURVIN** (B2672). 1907: Sold to Société Ervin, Boulogne.
1908: Sold to E Canu, Boulogne. 1921: Sold to Soc Gen D'Armement, Boulogne.
1922: Sold to Soc Nouvelle des Pêcheries à Vapeur, Arcachon. 1935: Sold to M Farine, Arcachon,
1936: Transferred to Bordeaux. 06.1936: Stranded. No further details.

BRAZILIAN	261 (B)	176	110.8	Great Central Co-op	Great Central Co-op
110914 Iron built	10.08.1899	68	21.0	46 rhp 3-cyl	Engineering & Ship Repair
GY888 steam trawler	11.1899		10.8	10.0 knots	Co Ltd, Grimsby

03.11.1899: Registered at Grimsby (GY888). 06.1901: Sold to Delpyere, Boulogne, France. 03.07.1901: Grimsby registry closed.
07.1901: Renamed **FAIDHERBE** (B-2732). 1902: Wrecked off Penmarc'h, Finistère. Salved and repaired.
08.1903: Re-classed and sold to Pinchon, Boulogne. 1906: Sold to A H Peigue, Nantes, and renamed **HARLE** (N1691).
1907: Sold to M Gomez Hijo, Santiago de Cuba, Cuba, and renamed **ORIENTE**.
1911: Removed from Lloyd's Register of Shipping. No further details.

SARDIUS	262 (S)	206	116.2	C D Holmes	Arctic Steam Fishing
110937 Iron built	21.09.1899	70	21.0	53 rhp 3-cyl	Co Ltd,
GY1140 steam trawler	25.01.1899		11.5	10.0 knots	Grimsby

26.01.1900: Registered at Grimsby (GY1140). 06.1915: Requisitioned for war service as a minesweeper (1-3pdr) (Ad.No. 3357).
08.1915: Renamed **SARDIUS II**. 12.02.1918: Rounding Runnelstone Buoy (light extinguished) for Mounts Bay, struck Runnelstone
Rock at 2345. 13.02.1918: Badly holed and settling, drifted into Pendower Cove, 1 mile north of Tol-Pedn-Penwith and drove ashore
at 0038 becoming a total wreck. Crew had taken to boat and picked up by trawler KONG FREDERICK (Ad.No.2659) (GY482)
(260grt/1909) and landed in Penzance. 16.04.1919: Grimsby registry closed - "Vessel lost".

BROUGH	263 (B)	205	118.4	C D Holmes	James Henry Collinson,
110774 Iron built steam	20.11.1899	64	21.5	63 rhp 3-cyl	Hull
H493 trawler	13.02.1899		11.5	10.0 knots	

11.04.1900: Registered at Hull (H493). 12.02.1905: In heavy snow storm, stranded on Reykjarnes, Stranda, north-west coast of
Iceland. 02.03.1905: Hull registry closed - "Totally wrecked".

AMESBURY ABBEY	264 (S)	202	115.5	Tindall, Earle & Hutchinson	Abbey Steam Fishing
113167 Iron built	20.11.1899	70	21.5	60 rhp 3-cyl	Co Ltd,
GY1160 steam trawler	02.04.1900		11.5	10.0 knots	Grimsby

06.04.1900: Registered at Grimsby (GY1160). 18.01.1908: Foundered 235 miles E by N of Spurn Point following collision with
trawler FALSTAFF (H917) (173grt/1906). 22.01.1908: Grimsby registry closed - "Sunk in North Sea".

BATTLE ABBEY	265 (S)	202	115.5	Tindall, Earle & Hutchinson	Abbey Steam Fishing
113177 Iron built	04.01.1899	74	21.5	60 rhp 3-cyl	Co Ltd,
GY1171 steam trawler	26.05.1900		11.5	10.0 knots	Grimsby

28.05.1900: Registered at Grimsby (GY1171). 1913: New boiler fitted. 11.1913: Sold to Samuel Gidley, Grimsby.
01.1916: Sold to John L Green, Grimsby. 17.08.1916: Sold to Cleethorpes Steam Trawling Co Ltd, Grimsby.
16.06.1917: Grimsby registry closed - "Sunk in collision". Salved and repaired. 11.1918: Sold to Robert D Clarke, Grimsby.
29.11.1918: Renamed **ENSIGN** (GY1216). 05.1925: Sold to Gerald de Yandiola, Bilbao, Spain.
13.05.1925: Grimsby registry closed. 05.1925: Renamed **JUAN MARI No. 2**, registered at San Sebastián. Re-measured to 113.5ft;
tonnages amended to 209grt, 92net. 1933: Sold to Antonia de Zárraga, Bilbao.
1950: Sold to Herdores de Antonia de Zárraga, Bilbao. 1954: Sold to Ma Rosario Yandiola y Zárraga & others, San Sebastián.
1966: Sold for breaking up.

HARRIER 113198 Iron built steam GY1192 trawler	266 (S) 16.06.1900 09.08.1900	208 83	117.0 21.5 11.2	C D Holmes 60 rhp 3-cyl 10.0 knots	Thomas Baskcomb, Grimsby

03.08.1900: Registered at Grimsby (GY1192).   23.04.1914: Sold to Mary A Baskcomb, Thomas W Baskcomb, John C Store & Herbert Crabtree, Grimsby.   24.08.1914: Stopped in North Sea by German torpedo boat and sunk by explosive charges; crew taken prisoner.   09.11.1914: Grimsby registry closed - "Blown up by enemy".

GOSHAWK 113200 Iron built steam GY1194 trawler	267 (S) 28.06.1900 25.08.1900	208 83	117.0 21.5 11.2	C D Holmes 60 rhp 3-cyl 10.0 knots	Thomas Baskcomb, Grimsby

25.08.1900: Registered at Grimsby (GY1194).   23.04.1914: Sold to Mary A Baskcomb, Thomas W Baskcomb, John C Store & Herbert Crabtree, Grimsby.   19.10.1915: Sold to Thomas Baskcomb Ltd, Grimsby.
12.1914: Requisitioned for war service as a minesweeper (1-6pdr) (Ad.No.430).   13.04.1915: Renamed **GOSHAWK II** (GY1194).
1919: Returned.   12.07.1933: Company re-styled Amalgamated Steam Fishing Co Ltd, Grimsby.   02.1935: Sold for breaking up.
22.2.1935: Grimsby registry closed.

ST LOUIS 110798 Iron built steam H503 trawler	268 (B) 03.04.1900 24.05.1900	239 83	125.7 21.6 11.8	C D Holmes 70 rhp 3-cyl 10.5 knots	Thomas Hamling & Co Ltd, Hull

26.05.1900: Registered at Hull (H503).   12.1914: Requisitioned for war service as a minesweeper (1-6pdr) (Ad.No.1202).
1919: Returned.   11.1923: Sold to W J Kermer Jnr, IJmuiden, Holland.   20.11.1923: Hull registry closed.
11.1923: Renamed **CORRIE** (IJM21). Tonnages re-measured to 229grt, 80net.
02.1927: Sold to N V Nordzee Exploitatie Maats, IJmuiden.   1928: Sold to N V Vissch Maats Corrie, IJmuiden.
26.03.1942: Sunk in the North Sea by Royal Navy motor torpedo boats.

KING HAAKON 110942 Iron built GY1145 steam trawler	269 (S) 01.02.1900 10.03.1900	239 54	117.2 21.6 12.0	Amos & Smith 66 rhp 3-cyl 10.5 knots	Viking Steam Fishing Co Ltd, Grimsby

12.03.1900: Registered at Grimsby (GY1145).   10.1902: Sold to Soc Immobilière du Moulleau et des Pêcheries de l'Océan, Arcachon.   20.10.1902: Grimsby registry closed.   10.1902: Renamed **GOELAND** (ARC8951).   1910: Transferred to Bordeaux.
1915: Commissioned in Marine Française as a minesweeper.   04.01.1918: Stopped by U-boat (U 93) off Penmarc'h, Finistère, while on passage from Brest towards Lézardrieux and sunk.

KING OLAV 113165 Iron built GY1158 steam trawler	270 (S) 17.02.1900 24.03.1900	235 54	117.2 21.6 12.0	Amos & Smith 66 rhp 3-cyl 10.5 knots	Viking Steam Fishing Co Ltd, Grimsby

26.03.1900: Registered at Grimsby (GY1158).   10.1902: Sold to Soc Immobilière du Moulleau et des Pêcheries de l'Océan, Arcachon.   20.10.1902: Grimsby registry closed.   10.1902: Renamed **MOUETTE** (ARC8950).   1910: Transferred to Bordeaux.
1920: Sold to Soc des Pêcheries de l'Océan, Bordeaux.   1929: Removed from Lloyd's Register of Shipping.

WINDSOR CASTLE 110703 Iron built steam H49 trawler	271 (1) 14.02.1899 01.05.1899	189 54	115.0 21.1 11.0	Shanks Anderson 73 nhp 3-cyl 10.5 knots	James A Smith Steam Trawling Co Ltd Hull

Commenced by D Macgill (Yard No. 1) in the former yard of Donaldson, Aiken & Scott, Govan; completed by Cochrane & Cooper Ltd, Govan.   01.05.1899: Registered at Hull (H49).   09.1903: Sold to Hubert et Cie, Dieppe, France.
08.09.1903: Hull registry closed.   09.1903: Renamed **ALCYON** (D1433).   1908: Sold to G Vallée, Dieppe.
1913: Sold to Russian Murman Steam Fishing Co Ltd, Archangel, Russia. Renamed **WOSTOCK**.
1915: Commissioned by Russian authorities and renamed **T.6**.   03.08.1918: One of seventeen Russian trawlers seized in the North Sea and acquired by the British Government from the 'White' Russian authority.   Commissioned into the Royal Navy and renamed **GREATAXE** (Ad.No.4340).   11.05.1920: Sold to John Lewis Ltd, Aberdeen.   15.07.1920: Registered at Aberdeen as **GREATAXE** (A371).   1923: Sold to William Masson & others, Aberdeen.   23.04.1925: Renamed **ROSLIN** (A371).   04.11.1937: At about 9.00pm in steadily worsening weather conditions, stranded approximately 200 – 300 yards south of the mouth of the River Ythan on the Aberdeenshire coast. Aberdeen lifeboat rescued two crew but six members were lost.
28.01.1938: Aberdeen registry closed - "Total loss".

BALMORAL CASTLE 100726 Iron built steam H466 trawler	272 (2) 08.04.1899 08.07.1899	189 52	115.0 21.0 11.0	Shanks Anderson 60 nhp 3-cyl 10.0 knots	James A Smith Steam Trawling Co Ltd Hull

Commenced by D Macgill (Yard No. 2) in the former yard of Donaldson, Aiken & Scott, Govan; completed by Cochrane & Cooper Ltd, Govan.   10.07.1899: Registered at Hull (H466).   11.07.1903: Sold to Soc Immobilière du Moulleau et des Pêcheries de l'Océan, Arcachon, France.   13.07.1903: Hull registry closed.   07.1903: Renamed **ALCYON** (ARC9109).
1918: Removed from Lloyd's Register of Shipping - war loss.

VALIANT 113183 Iron built GY1178 steam trawler	273 (B) 18.04.1900 18.06.1900	198 75	113.0 21.5 11.2	C D Holmes 55 rhp 3-cyl 10.0 knots	Atlas Steam Fishing Co Ltd, Grimsby

19.06.1900: Registered at Grimsby (GY1178).   25.08.1914: Stopped in North Sea off Whitby by German torpedo boats and sunk by explosive charges; crew taken prisoner.   11.09.1914: Grimsby registry closed.

Cochrane & Cooper Ltd, Selby. (All vessels built at Selby)

RODRIGO 113214 Iron built GY1208 steam trawler	290 25.10.1900 26.11.1900	169 60	101.0 21.0 11.0	C D Holmes 55 rhp 3-cyl 10.0 knots	George F Sleight, Grimsby
03.12.1900: Registered at Grimsby (GY1208). 1917: Requisitioned for Fishery Reserve. 1919: Released. 11. 1938: Sold to Consolidated Fisheries Ltd, Grimsby. 23.11.1938: Grimsby registry closed. 26.11.1938: Registered at Lowestoft (LT252). 06.12.1938: Transferred to Lowestoft. 15.12.1938: Renamed **FRAMLINGHAM** (LT252). 03.10.1940: Survived an attack by German aircraft 20 miles south of Fastnet. 1944: Sold to Charles Dobson, Grimsby. 1944: Lowestoft registry closed. Registered at Grimsby (GY1). 1945: Sold to Elkington Estates Ltd, Grimsby. 1947: Sold to Respondo Trawlers Ltd, Milford Haven. 10.03.1952: Sold to BISCO and allocated to Thos W Ward Ltd, Sheffield, for breaking up at Castle Pill, Milford Haven. 03.1952: Grimsby registry closed.					
RESTO 113215 Iron built GY1209 steam trawler	291 22.11.1900 14.12.1900	169 59	101.0 21.3 11.0	C D Holmes 55 rhp 3-cyl 10.0 knots	George F Sleight, Grimsby
03.01.1901: Registered at Grimsby (GY1209). 25.02.1915: Posted missing whilst on a North Sea trip. No survivors. 17.05.1915: Grimsby registry closed - "Missing".					
No. 3 Not registered Iron built water boat	292 1900 06.12.1900		45.0 13.3	E F & R Turner	G R Sanderson & Co Ltd, Grimsby

Cochrane & Sons, Selby. (All vessels built at Selby)

PERSIA 114832 Iron built steam tug	293 30.10.1901 20.01.1902	146 9	94.0 19.6 11.0	J Stewart & Son 99 rhp 3-cyl	William Watkins, London
1906: Foundered having been damaged by the screw of P&O steamer MARMORA (10509grt/1903). Salved and repaired. 1907: New high pressure cylinder fitted. 11.04.1908: Foundered 3 miles north-east of Sunk light-vessel, Thames estuary, following collision in fog with steamer HUGUENOT (1032grt/1892), approximate position 51º 48.8'N, 001º 34'E.					
No. 13 121026 Iron built lighter	294 1902 20.01.1902	118 115	74.7 19.6 8.7	N/A	Joseph Rank, Hull
30.01.1905: Registered at Hull. 13.08.1913: Hull registry closed, transferred to Liverpool. 12.04.1921: Sold to B J Transport Co Ltd, London. Still registered in 1956.					
No. 14 121027 Iron built lighter	295 1902 20.01.1902	118 115	74.7 19.6 8.7	N/A	Joseph Rank, Hull
30.01.1905: Registered at Hull. 13.08.1913: Hull registry closed, transferred to Liverpool. 12.04.1921: Sold to B J Transport Co Ltd, London. Still registered in 1956.					
No. 1 Wood barge	296 24.05.1902 03.06.1902	192 192	60.0 22.0	N/A	Watts, Watts & Co Ltd, London
No. 2 Wood barge	297 24.05.1902 03.06.1902	192 192	60.0 22.0	N/A	Watts, Watts & Co Ltd, London
No. 3 Wood barge	298 09.07.1902 23.07.1902	192 192	60.0 22.0	N/A	Watts, Watts & Co Ltd, London
No. 4 Wood barge	299 09.07.1902 23.07.1902	192 192	60.0 22.0	N/A	Watts, Watts & Co Ltd, London
No. 5 Wood barge	300 04.09.1902 11.09.1902	192 192	60.0 22.0	N/A	Watts, Watts & Co Ltd, London
No. 6 Wood barge	301 04.09.1902 11.09.1902	192 192	60.0 22.0	N/A	Watts, Watts & Co Ltd, London

Kimberley (302)

(Jonathan Grobler collection)

KIMBERLEY 113227 Steam trawler GY1227	302 09.06.1902 26.07.1902	190 73	110.5 21.5 11.2	C D Holmes 55 rhp 3-cyl 10.0 knots	H L Taylor & H Bernstein, Grimsby

28.07.1902: Registered at Grimsby (GY1227).   11.1904: Sold to Norway.   11.11.1904: Grimsby registry closed.
08.1906: Sold to H L Taylor, Grimsby.   09.08.1906: Registered at Grimsby (GY167).   04.1910: Sold to H L Taylor & R Staff, Grimsby.
08.1914: Requisitioned for war service as a minesweeper (1-12pdr) (Ad.No.11).   1919: Returned.
12.1919: Sold to H L Taylor & H G Hopwood, Grimsby.   10.1922: Sold to Diamonds Steam Fishing Co Ltd, Grimsby.
11.1939: Requisitioned for war service as a minesweeper; hire rate £47.10.0d per month.   12.1939: Renamed **MANLY**.
14.02.1940: Returned and reverted to **KIMBERLEY** (GY167).   29.03.1941: On passage from Grimsby to Hartlepool, foundered
22 miles south-east of Flamborough Head after being bombed by German aircraft. All nine crew saved.
26.08.1941: Grimsby registry closed.

CAVE 116085 Steam trawler H643	303 08.07.1902 15.09.1902	247 93	125.0 21.5 12.0	C D Holmes 70 rhp 3-cyl 11.0 knots	James Henry Collinson, Hull

One of the first trawlers built with a whale back and veranda bridge. 17.09.1902: Registered at Hull (H643).
11.1914: Requisitioned for war service as a minesweeper (1-12pdr, 1-6pdr HA) (Ad.No. 389).   1919: Returned.
23.10.1923: Sold to executors of late James H Collinson - Harry Collinson, Henry Hewitt & Jesse Spring, Hull.
02.07.1924: Sold to Harry, Stanley & Charles Collinson, Hull.   10.10.1924: Sold to Harry & Stanley Collinson, Hull.
10.08.1933: Sold to Dalby Steam Fishing Co Ltd, Fleetwood.   15.07.1943: Sold to J Bennett (Wholesale) Ltd, London.
21.10.1946: Sold to Ocean Fishing Co, Newhaven, Edinburgh.   07.11.1947: Sold to Joseph Croan, Edinburgh.
12.08.1948: Sold to Den Fishing Co Ltd, Dundee.
1950: Sold to BISCO and allocated to P & W McLellan Ltd, Bo'ness, for breaking up.   03.05.1950: Arrived Bo'ness.
22.12.1950: Hull registry closed on advice the ship had been broken up.

THISTLE 113234 Steam trawler GY1234	304 20.08.1902 11.10.1902	167 40	102.4 20.7 10.7	C D Holmes 56 rhp 3-cyl 10.0 knots	Charles A Osborne, Grimsby

14.10.1902: Registered at Grimsby (GY1234).   29.01.1917: Stopped by U-boat (UC31) 140 miles NE byN1/2N off mouth of River
Tyne and sunk. Crew escaped.   07.03.1917: Grimsby registry closed.

IONA 116095 Lighter	305 02.10.1902 16.10.1902	124 124	72.0 21.0 10.9	N/A	John A Scott, Hull

23.10.1902: Registered at Hull.   15.07.1958: Sold to Cranfield Brothers Ltd, Ipswich.   13.01.1976: Sold for breaking up.

STAFFA 116096 Lighter	306 02.10.1902 16.10.1902	124 124	72.0 21.0 10.9	N/A	John A Scott, Hull

23.10.1902: Registered at Hull.   15.07.1958: Sold to Cranfield Brothers Ltd, Ipswich.   13.01.1976: Sold for breaking up.

MIRA 115921 Steam tug	307 20.09.1902 10.11.1902	50 2	62.8 14.9 7.4	Tindall Earle & Hutchinson 24 rhp 2-cyl 10.0 knots	Wilson, Sons & Co Ltd, London

11.1902: Registered at London.   1911: London registry closed. Deleted from Mercantile Navy List.

POWERFUL 116130 Steam tug	308 03.11.1902 20.02.1902	195 6	114.0 21.1 12.0	Tindall Earle & Hutchinson 98 rhp 3-cyl 12.0 knots	John S Darrell & Robert H James, St George's, Bermuda

21.03.1903: Registered at Hull.   16.04.1903: Transferred to Bermuda.   05.06.1903: Hull registry closed. Registered at Hamilton.
1936: Sold to Darrell & Meyer Ltd, Hamilton, Bermuda.   1940: Vessel removed from Lloyd's Register of Shipping.

NORA 115914 Steam tug	309 20.09.1902 26.10.1902	50 2	62.8 14.9 7.4	Tindall Earle & Hutchinson 24 rhp 2-cyl 10.0 knots	Wilson, Sons & Co Ltd, London

22.10.1902: Registered at London.   1930: Deleted from Mercantile Navy List.

Drax *(331)*

(Authors' collection)

Gurth *(332)*

(Jonathan Grobler collection)

Leo *(333)*

(Jonathan Grobler collection)

INGOMAR 118934 Steam trawler GY32	326 16.08.1904 09.1904	217 80	115.0 21.5 11.5	Great Central Co-op 60 rhp 3-cyl 10.0 knots	Edwin Bacon, Grimsby

04.10.1904: Registered at Grimsby (GY32).   11.1906: Sold to Dolphin Steam Fishing Co Ltd, Grimsby.
09.1915: Sold to Arctic Steam Fishing Co Ltd, Grimsby.   29.05.1917: Requisitioned for Fishery Reserve.   1919: Released.
07.1930: Sold to G Bacon, Grimsby.   10.1930: Sold to T C & F Moss, Grimsby.   04.1931: Renamed **CONISTON** (GY32).
29.11.1939: Requisitioned for war service as a minesweeper (P. No. FY.833); hire rate £54.5.0d per month.
06.02.1940: Returned to owner.   1955: Sold to Belgian shipbreakers.   07.11.1955: Arrived at Boom for demolition.
11.1955: Grimsby registry closed.

JAPAN 118932 Steam trawler GY28	327 16.07.1904 08.1904	205 78	114.0 21.6 11.2	C D Holmes 60 rhp 3-cyl 10.0 knots	Henry Lewis Taylor, Grimsby

26.08.1904: Registered at Grimsby (GY28).   08.1914: Requisitioned for war service as a minesweeper (Ad.No.42).
16.08.1915: Mined off the south end of the Shipwash Shoal while 'sweeping with the TOUCHSTONE (H934) (Ad.No.46). Whilst clearing the sweep, a mine was spotted about 30 yards away, foul of JAPAN's sweep wire; heaving stopped but the mine had submerged with the tide; detonated 10 seconds later and JAPAN sank within 30 seconds. Five crew lost.
26.10.1915: Grimsby registry closed.

MONARCH 118935 Steam trawler GY29	328 29.08.1904 10.1904	234 107	120.0 22.0 11.6	C D Holmes 60 rhp 3-cyl 10.0 knots	Monarch Steam Fishing Co Ltd, Grimsby

15.10.1904: Registered at Grimsby (GY29).   1908: Sold to Anchor Steam Fishing Co Ltd, Grimsby.
07.1915: Requisitioned for war service as a minesweeper (1-12pdr, 1-7.5" A/S Howitzer) (AD.No.1599).
08.1915: Renamed **MONARCH III**.   30.8.1918: Sold to J Little, Grimsby. Registered at Grimsby as **MONARCH III** (GY29).
1919: Returned.   13.03.1919: Sold to Brent Steam Fishing Co Ltd, Grimsby.   13.01.1925: Sold to Francis Victor Vokes, Filey.
12.01.1925: Grimsby registry closed.   13.01.1925: Registered at Hull (H118).   20.02.1925: Renamed **GOLDEN GLEAM** (H118).
18.12.1925: Sold to Edith Crimlis, Filey.   07.01.1930: Sold to Francis Crimlis, Hull.
04.09.1930: Sold to Richard Ferguson Cammish, Filey.   10.1936: Sold to shipbreakers and broken up at Stockton on Tees.
19.10.1936: Hull registry closed.

RELIANCE 118936 Steam trawler GY30	329 27.09.1904 11.1904	203 83	115.0 21.6 11.3	C D Holmes 58 rhp 3-cyl 10.0 knots	Edward C Grant, Grimsby

08.11.1904: Registered at Grimsby (GY30).   10.1910: Sold to Thomas W Baskcomb, Grimsby.
12.1914: Requisitioned for war service as a minesweeper (1-6pdr) (Ad.No.999).   02.1915: Renamed **RELIANCE II** (GY30).
1919: Returned.   03.1916: Sold to Earl Steam Fishing Co Ltd, Grimsby.   11.08.1916: Sold to H Croft Baker, Grimsby.
01.1923: Sold to Savoy Steam Fishing Co Ltd, Grimsby.   08.1928: Sold to Fred Bacon, Grimsby.
09.1939: Sold to shipbreakers in Belgium and broken up.   04.09.1939: Grimsby registry closed.

MANXMAN 118937 Steam trawler GY34	330 12.10.1904 11.1904	196 76	115.5 21.5 11.4	C D Holmes 60 rhp 3-cyl 10.0 knots	Walter H Beeley & Blanchard, Grimsby

16.11.1904: Registered at Grimsby (GY34).   04.1911: Sold to South Western Steam Fishing Co Ltd, Grimsby & Fleetwood.
04.1912: Sold to Marshall Line Steam Fishing Co Ltd, Grimsby.   12.1912: Sold to Thomas W Baskcomb, Grimsby, & others.
09.1915: Sold to Sleights Steam Fishing Co Ltd, Grimsby.   14.04.1917: Stranded on Westmann Isles, Iceland.
14.05.1917: Grimsby registry closed.

DRAX 121013 Steam trawler H733	331 09.11.1904 09.01.1905	272 94	132.0 22.0 12.3	C D Holmes 70 rhp 3-cyl 10.5 knots	James Henry Collinson, Hull

10.01.1905: Registered at Hull (H733).   16.08.1913: Struck a rock in Faxa Bay, Iceland, and foundered in deep water.
09.09.1913: Hull registry closed - "Ship a total loss".

GURTH 118941 Steam trawler GY39	332 10.12.1904 01.1905	226 91	123.2 21.6 11.4	C D Holmes 60 rhp 3-cyl 10.0 knots	United Steam Fishing Co Ltd, Grimsby

27.01.1905: Registered at Grimsby (GY39).   10.1914 Requisitioned for war service as a minesweeper (1-12pdr) (Ad.No. 663).
1919: Returned.   1955: Sold to Van Heyghen Frères, Ghent, Belgium, for breaking up.   12.1955: Arrived Ghent.
12.1955: Grimsby registry closed.

LEO 118939 Steam trawler GY36	333 12.11.1904 01.1905	181 61	110.0 21.0 10.9	Great Central Co-op 45 rhp 3-cyl 9.5 knots	Grimsby & North Sea Steam Fishing Co Ltd, Grimsby

04.01.1905: Registered at Grimsby (GY36).   29.05.1917: Requisitioned for Fishery Reserve.   1919: Released.
08.1921: Sold to Lindsey Steam Fishing Co Ltd, Grimsby.
29.12.1942: On a North Sea trip, left Scrabster for Grimsby and last seen at 6.00pm NE by N of Kinnaird Head in a whole NN-E gale and snow. No survivors from eleven crew.   29.05.1943: Grimsby registry closed.

St George (344) *under later name of* **Cedric**

(Jonathan Grobler collection)

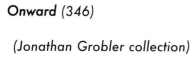

Onward (346)

(Jonathan Grobler collection)

Cyrano (347)

(Jonathan Grobler collection)

EMERALD	341	209	115.0	C D Holmes	Robert Cole, Erel E Carter
121601 Steam trawler	08.04.1905	66	21.6	60 rhp 3-cyl	& Barnard H Galvin,
M37	06.06.1905		11.9	10.0 knots	Milford Haven

25.05.1905: Registered at Milford (M37). 1 7.02.1910: Sold to Robert Cole, Erel E Carter & David G Jones, Milford Haven.
12.09.1911: Sold to Robert Cole & David G Jones, Milford Haven. 19.01.1917: Sold to George F Sleight, Grimsby.
20.01.1917: Milford registry closed. 29.01.1917: Renamed **RESPONDO** (GY1019). 29.05.1917: Requisitioned for Fishery Reserve.
1919: Released. 1921: Sold to the executors of Sir George F Sleight, Bart, Grimsby.
11.1933: Sold to Doris Burton Steam Trawling Co Ltd, Hartlepool. 07.11.1933: Grimsby registry closed.
11.1933: Registered at Hartlepool (HL63). 1937: Sold to R H Davison & Co Ltd, Hartlepool.
10.05.1940: Sold to Respondo Trawlers Ltd, Milford Haven.
1.09.1940: Sailed Milford for Irish grounds; skipper Thomas Owston; eleven crew.
11.09.1940: Presumed lost off Old Head of Kinsale. No survivors. 01.10.1940: Posted missing - cause unknown or uncertain.
11.1940: Hartlepool registry closed.

CLITUS	342	240	123.6	Great Central Co-op	Orient Steam Fishing
122691 Steam trawler	22.04.1905	98	22.0	70 rhp 3-cyl	Co Ltd,
GY63	23.06.1905		11.5	10.5 knots	Grimsby

24.06.1905: Registered at Grimsby (GY63). 15.04.1908: Vessel foundered one mile off the east pierhead, Blyth Harbour.
29.05.1908: Grimsby registry closed.

JANUS	343	240	123.6	Great Central Co-op	Orient Steam Fishing
122692 Steam trawler	08.05.1905	98	22.0	70 rhp 3-cyl	Co Ltd,
GY64	05.08.1905		11.5	10.5 knots	Grimsby

24.06.1905: Registered at Grimsby (GY64). 08.1914: Requisitioned for war service as a minesweeper (1-3pdr) (Ad.No.325).
12.1914: Renamed **JANUS II** (GY64). 1920: Returned. 02.1920: Sold to Direct Fish Supplies Ltd, London.
23.03.1922: Direct Fish Supplies Ltd in voluntary liquidation. 10.08.1922: Placed in compulsory liquidation.
09.1922: Sold to Thomas W Baskcomb, Grimsby. 22.10.1935: Fleet of Thomas W Baskcomb sold to Fred Parkes, Blackpool.
04.1936: Sold to shipbreakers and broken up. 22.04.1936: Grimsby registry closed.

ST GEORGE	344	229	123.6	C D Holmes	Grimsby Victor Steam
122702 Steam trawler	19.07.1905	94	22.0	63 rhp 3-cyl	Fishing Co Ltd,
GY83	09.09.1905		11.5	10.0 knots	Grimsby

06.09.1905: Registered at Grimsby (GY83). 02.1915: Requisitioned for war service as a minesweeper (1-6pdr HA) (Ad.No.688).
11.1917: Sold to Ernest Taylor, Fleetwood. 30.11.1917: Renamed **LORD GEORGE** (GY83).
11.09.1918: Sold to Ernest Taylor & Noah Ashworth, Fleetwood. 11.01.1919: Returned. 18.07.1919: Grimsby registry closed.
20.07.1919: Registered at Fleetwood (FD329). 8.1919: Sold to Ernest Taylor, Thornton. 1925: Sold to Italian owners.
31.3.1925: Fleetwood registry closed. 08.1926: Sold to Mrs Laura Watson, Cleveleys. 10.08.1926: Renamed **JOHN-ERIK** (FD52).
12.1926: Sold to United Steam Fishing Co Ltd, Grimsby. 30.12.1926: Fleetwood registry closed.
12.01.1927: Registered at Grimsby (GY420). 01.1927: Renamed **CEDRIC** (GY420).
29.11.1939: Requisitioned for war service as a minesweeper (P. No. FY.996); hire rate £57.10.0d per month.
05.1940: Fitted out as a barrage balloon vessel. Based at Scapa Flow. 31.04.1947: Sold to The Admiralty.
05.1947: Sold to J R Hepworth & Co (Hull) Ltd and broken up at Paull, near Hull. 10.1947: Grimsby registry closed.

PRESIDENT STEVENS	345	212	115.0	C D Holmes	Soc Anon des Pêcheries à
Steam trawler	03.08.1905	87	21.5	69 nhp 3-cyl	Vapeur,
O85	21.09.1905		11.7	11.7 knots	Ostend, Belgium

09.1905: Registered at Ostend (O85). 1906: Sold to J Bauwens, Ostend. 1910: Sold to Soc Anon des Pêcheries à Vapeur, Ostend.
1924: Sold to Madame Yvonne Carimantrant, Paris, France, and renamed **ADINE**. 1931: Sold to J Delpierre, Boulogne.
1936: Sold to Jean Fourmentin-Delpierre, Boulogne. 1956: Sold to shipbreakers in France and broken up.

ONWARD	346	209	115.0	C D Holmes	Forward Steam Fishing
122705 Steam trawler	02.09.1905	73	21.6	60 rhp 3-cyl	Co Ltd,
GY87	25.10.1905		11.5	10.0 knots	Grimsby

19.10.1905: Registered at Grimsby (GY87). 27.11.1939: Requisitioned for war service as a minesweeper (P. No.FY.887); hire rate
£52.5.0d per month. 31.01.1940: Returned. 08.1956: Sold to Louis Appel & Co, the Netherlands, for breaking up.
19.09.1956: Arrived Dordrecht. 10.1956: Grimsby registry closed.

CYRANO	347	214	117.0	C D Holmes	Alick Black,
122699 Steam trawler	19.06.1905	77	21.6	60 rhp 3-cyl	Grimsby
GY80	20.08.1905		11.7	10.0 knots	

04.08.1905: Registered at Grimsby (GY80). Fishing from Fleetwood. 04.1914: Sold to Strand Steam Fishing Co Ltd, Grimsby.
06.1915: Requisitioned for war service as a minesweeper (1-12pdr) (Ad.No.1528). Based Penzance. 1919: Returned.
13.08.1919: Posted missing on a North Sea trip. No survivors. 04.10.1919: Grimsby registry closed - "Missing".

Pelican (349)

(Barnard & Straker collection)

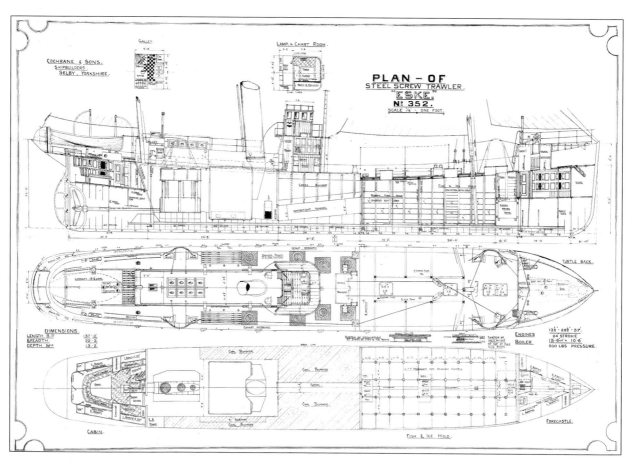

A general arrangement drawing of the **Eske** (352)

ROMILLY	348	214	117.0	C D Holmes	John L Green,
122701 Steam trawler	04.07.1905	77	21.6	60 rhp 3-cyl	Grimsby
GY81	31.08.1905		11.7	10.0 knots	

22.08.1905: Registered at Grimsby (GY81).   07.1914: Sold to Denmark.   14.07.1914: Grimsby registry closed.
03.1915: Sold to John L Green, Grimsby.   10.03.1915: Registered at Grimsby (GY437).
03.1915: Requisitioned for war service as a minesweeper (1-12pdr) (Ad.No.2651).   1919: Returned.
11.1925: Sold to Harold Bacon, Grimsby.   09.1930: Sold to Kottingham Trawling Co Ltd, Grimsby.
01.1945: Sold to Parkholme Trawlers Ltd, Fleetwood.   06.1945: Sold to Rushcliffe Trawlers Ltd, Grimsby.
04.1948: Sold to Ravendale Trawlers Ltd, Grimsby.   11.1952: Sold to Saint Andrew's Steam Fishing Co Ltd, Hull.
06.1954: Sold to BISCO and allocated to J J King & Co Ltd, Gateshead.   10.1955: Grimsby registry closed.

PELICAN	349	205	114.0	C D Holmes	Cleethorpes Steam Trawler
122707 Steam trawler	16.09.1905	73	21.6	60 rhp 3-cyl	Co Ltd,
GY91	08.11.1905		11.2	10.0 knots	Grimsby

09.11.1905: Registered at Grimsby (GY91).   07.1916: Requisitioned for war service as a minesweeper (1-12pdr) (Ad.No.3265);
renamed **PELICAN II**.   1920: Returned and reverted to **PELICAN** (GY91).   16.04.1918: Sold to A Beeley, Grimsby.
29.04.1919: Sold to Sleights Steam Fishing Co Ltd, Grimsby.   01.1939: Sold to Premier Steam Fishing Co Ltd, Grimsby.
10.1941: Sold to Sir Alec Black, Bart, Grimsby.   04.1943: Sold to Grimsby Motor Trawlers Ltd, Grimsby.
01.04.1944: Requisitioned war service as a smoke making trawler. Renamed **ERIDANES** (P. No. 4.427); hire rate £51.5.0d per month.
03.11.1944: Returned and reverted to **PELICAN** (GY91).   10.1945: Sold to Ravendale Trawlers Ltd, Grimsby.
1951: Sold to BISCO and allocated Clayton & Davie Ltd, Dunston, for breaking up.
05.11.1951: Arrived River Tyne under tow from Grimsby.   05.1952: Grimsby registry closed.

EMPEROR	350	250	127.0	C D Holmes	Anchor Steam Fishing
122710 Steam trawler	02.10.1905	105	22.1	70 rhp 3-cyl	Co Ltd,
GY94	04.12.1905		11.5	10.5 knots	Grimsby

02.12.1905: Registered at Grimsby (GY94).   11.1914: Requisitioned for war service (1-3pdr, 1-2pdr) (Ad.No.685).
20.01.1915: Renamed **MEROR** (GY94).   1920: Returned.   03.1923: Sold to Trawlers White Sea & Grimsby Co Ltd, Grimsby.
27.05.1930: Stranded between the Bull Lightship and Spurn Point following a collision with the German steam coaster
DORA AHRENS (858grt/1901).   09.09.1930: Grimsby registry closed - "Total Loss".
10.1930: Salved and sold to J S Doig, Grimsby. Repaired.   01.11.1930: Registered at Grimsby (GY316).
11.1930: Sold to A & E Grant, Grimsby.   04.1931: Sold to Arthur Grant & Son Ltd, Grimsby.
05.09.1940: Requisitioned for war service as a minesweeper (P. No. FY.1836); hire rate £62.10.0d per month. Based Grimsby with
M/S Group 72.   03.10.1943: Mined in River Humber in approximate position 50° 08.6'N 001° 40.9'W. Ty/Skipper H J May, RNR, and
all crew saved.

CONCORD	351	235	120.7	C D Holmes	George W White &
122711 Steam trawler	14.10.1905	96	21.7	63 rhp 3-cyl	John N Willows,
GY95	09.12.1905		11.6	10.0 knots	Grimsby

06.12.1905: Registered at Grimsby (GY95).   12.1914: Requisitioned for service as a minesweeper (1-12pdr) (Ad.No.722).
12.1915: Renamed **CONCORD III**.   1919: Returned and reverted to **CONCORD** (GY95).
09.1925: Sold to Trawl A/B Kungshamn, Gothenburg, Sweden.   17.09.1925: Grimsby registry closed.
1948: Sold to Trål A/B Nordsjöm, Gothenburg.   1949: Sold to Rederi A/B Evernia, Gothenburg.
08.1949: Re-engined with 5cyl diesel by Harland & Wolff Ltd.   1951: Sold to Pontus Nilsson, Gothenburg. Renamed **GRÖNLAND**.
1952: Sold to Fiskeri A/B Grönland, Gothenburg. Renamed **TRUMAN**.
1953: Sold to Trygve Matland & Co A/S, Haugesund, Norway.   1957: Sold to shipbreakers and broken up.

ESKE	352	290	137.0	C D Holmes	James Henry Collinson,
123218 Steam trawler	31.10.1905	119	22.3	70 rhp 3-cyl	Hull
H859	16.01.1906		12.3	10.5 knots	

16.01.1906: Registered at Hull (H859).   02.1915: Requisitioned for war service as a minesweeper (1-6pdr, 1-7.5" A/S Howitzer)
(Ad.No.1225).   1919: Returned.
23.10.1923: Sold to executors of late J H Collinson: Harry Collinson, Henry Hewitt & Jesse Spring, Hull.
02.07.1924: Sold to Harry, Stanley & Charles Collinson, Hull.   10.09.1924: Sold to Harry & Stanley Collinson.
01.04.1930: Wrecked on Súlnasker, Vestmannaeyjar Isles, south coast of Iceland.   20.08.1930: Hull registry closed - "Total loss".

JAVA	353	128	94.0	G T Grey	William Watkins Ltd,
120611 "Seeking" steam	17.08.1905	6	19.6	99 rhp 3-cyl	London
tug	03.10.1905			11.0 knots	

Designed as a 'Seeking' tug which towed sailing ships out to sea from the River Thames, then searched for ships in need
of a tow, ranging as far afield as the Scilly Isles. When steam replaced sail, she worked in the London docks.
07.10.1905: Registered at London.   21.07.1914: Requisitioned for war service as a boarding tug; renamed **CARCASS** (P. No. N.62).
01.1918: Served in Downs boarding flotilla and Mediterranean (P. No. N.18).   14.05.1919: Returned and reverted to **JAVA**.
09.1939: Requisitioned for war service; miscellaneous naval duties; hire rate £75.0.0d per month.   08.10.1939: Port duties.
30.05.1940: At Dunkirk (W Jones, Master). Used own lifeboat to ferry troops from the beaches and brought home approximately 270
troops.   Subsequently employed on contraband patrol and later port duties.   08.12.1945: Returned.
02.1950: Sold to Ship Towage (London) Ltd, London.   05.1965: Sold to Canvey Island shipbreakers and stripped. Hulk resold to
Metaalhandel En Sloopwerken H P Heuvelman N V, Krimpen aan den IJssel, Netherlands, then to Belgian breakers.
05.03.1966: Hulk arrived at Bruges for breaking up.

Argonaut (384) was renamed ***Cloughstone*** in 1935. In this photograph she is arriving at Aberdeen on a date reported to be in April 1947. In the background is the Hall Russell shipyard with the Ellerman Wilson Line's steamer ***Carlo*** under construction and on the stocks Aberdeen's first new build motor trawler ***Star of Scotland***.

(Jonathan Grobler collection)

LORD NUNBURNHOLME	377	271	130.0	Amos & Smith	Yorkshire Steam Fishing
123278 Steam trawler	04.09.1906	98	22.3	84 rhp 3-cyl	Co Ltd,
H900	27.10.1906		11.9	11.0 knots	Hull

22.10.1906: Registered at Hull (H900).   05.1914: Sold to G Puls & Co, Oporto, Portugal.   08.05.1914: Hull registry closed.
Renamed **LORDELLO**.   1914: Believed to have been wrecked on the Portuguese coast.

FLAMINGO	378	271	130.0	Amos & Smith	Pickering & Haldane's
123279 Steam trawler	05.09.1906	98	22.3	84 rhp 3-cyl	Steam Trawling Co Ltd,
H901	08.11.1906		12.0	11.0 knots	Hull

02.11.1906: Registered at Hull (H901).   26.02.1911: Wrecked at Selvog, Iceland.   04.04.1911: Hull registry closed - "Total loss".

LADYSMITH	379	254	128.3	C D Holmes	Bernstein, Staff &
123596 Steam trawler	23.08.1906	109	22.0	69 rhp 3-cyl	Henry L Taylor,
GY183	07.12.1906		11.4	10.5 knots	Grimsby

07.12.1906: Registered at Grimsby (GY183).   08.1914: Requisitioned for war service as a minesweeper (1-12pdr HA) (Ad.No.4).
12.1919: Sold to H L Taylor & H G Hopwood, Grimsby.   1920: Returned.
10.1922: Sold to Diamonds Steam Fishing Co Ltd, Grimsby.   12.1929: Sold to Frank Crimlis, Hull.
13.12.1929: Grimsby registry closed.   14.12.1929: Registered at Hull (H167).   16.04.1930: Renamed **GOLDEN BEAM** (H167).
06.04.1934: Sold to Camloun Fishing Co Ltd, Aberdeen.   09.1937: Sold to shipbreakers in Germany and broken up.
24.09.1937: Hull registry closed.

AURORA	380	225	117.2	C D Holmes	Consolidated Steam
123586 Steam trawler	07.07.1906	106	22.0	67 rhp 3-cyl	Fishing & Ice Co Ltd,
GY172	16.10.1906		11.6	10.5 knots	Grimsby

17.10.1906: Registered at Grimsby (GY172).   08.1914: Requisitioned for war service as a minesweeper (1-6pdr HA) (Ad.No.345).
02.1915: Renamed **AURORA II**.   1919: Returned and reverted to **AURORA** (GY172).   10.1926: Sold to Charles Dobson, Grimsby.
04.1937: Sold for breaking up.   20.04.1937: Grimsby registry closed..

ARIADNE	381	225	117.2	C D Holmes	Consolidated Steam
123588 Steam trawler	24.07.1906	106	22.0	67 rhp 3-cyl	Fishing & Ice Co Ltd,
GY173	01.11.1906		11.6	10.5 knots	Grimsby

03.11.1906: Registered at Grimsby (GY173).   08.1914: Requisitioned for war service as a minesweeper (1-6pdr HA) (Ad.No.349).
02.1915: Renamed **ARIADNE II**.   11.1918: Returned and reverted to **ARIADNE** (GY173).
10.1926: Sold to Charles Dobson, Grimsby.   04.1937: Sold for breaking up.   20.04.1937: Grimsby registry closed.

ACHILLES	382	225	117.2	C D Holmes	Consolidated Steam
123592 Steam trawler	22.08.1906	106	22.0	67 rhp 3-cyl	Fishing & Ice Co Ltd,
GY182	22.11.1906		11.6	10.5 knots	Grimsby

23.11.1906: Registered at Grimsby (GY182).   08.1914: Requisitioned for war service as a minesweeper (1-6pdr) (Ad.No.293).
12.1915: Renamed **ACHILLES II**.   26.06.1918: Mined off Shipwash Light Vessel (mine laid on 25.06.1918 by UC.4).
16.04.1919: Grimsby registry closed.

AGAMEMNON	383	225	117.2	C D Holmes	Consolidated Steam
123598 Steam trawler	20.09.1906	106	22.0	67 rhp 3-cyl	Fishing & Ice Co Ltd,
GY187	03.01.1907		11.6	10.5 knots	Grimsby

07.01.1907: Registered at Grimsby (GY187).   08.1914: Requisitioned for war service as a minesweeper (Ad.No.19).
02.1915: Renamed **AGAMEMNON II**.   15.07.1915: Mined off Shipwash Light Vessel (mine laid the same day).
24.08.1915: Grimsby registry closed.

ARGONAUT	384	225	117.2	C D Holmes	Consolidated Steam
125044 Steam trawler	22.09.1906	106	22.0	67 rhp 3-cyl	Fishing & Ice Co Ltd,
GY189	29.01.1907		11.6	10.5 knots	Grimsby

30.01.1907: Registered at Grimsby (GY189).   09.1914: Captured by torpedo boat; crew taken prisoner.
14.09.1914: Grimsby registry closed.   1918: Released and returned.   1919: Sold to Boston Deep Sea Fishing & Ice Co Ltd, Boston.
Renamed **EWERBY** (BN158).   1921: Sold to Denos & Lebreton Tourasse & Co, Dieppe, France. Boston registry closed.
Renamed **JEAN-MAX**.   1935: Sold to James C Douglas, Aberdeen.   27.04.1935: Renamed **CLOUGHSTONE** (A257).
06.12.1940: Requisitioned for war service on balloon barrage (P. No. 4.446); hire rate £58.5.0d per month.
1942: Sold to Northern Trawlers Ltd, London.   04.1944: Converted to a smoke-making trawler.
09.06.1944: With Group A1 at Mulberry A, Normandy.   1944: Employed on miscellaneous naval duties.   28.04.1945: Returned.
12.1946: Sold to Lord Line Ltd, Hull.   12.1946: Aberdeen registry closed.   30.12.1946: Registered at Hull (H374).
21.01.1948: Sold to Milford Fisheries Ltd, Milford Haven.
1955: Sold to BISCO and allocated to T W Ward Ltd, Sheffield, for breaking up.   09.08.1955: Arrived at Grays, Essex.
02.03.1956: Hull registry closed.

VOLANTE	385	225	127.0	C D Holmes	Atlas Steam Fishing
125048 Steam trawler	18.10.1906	107	22.0	75 rhp 3-cyl	Co Ltd,
GY235	19.02.1907		11.6	10.5 knots	Grimsby

18.02.1907: Registered at Grimsby (GY235).   01.1915: Requisitioned for war service as a minesweeper (Ad.No.713).
06.11.1918: Sold to Harry Wood, Grimsby.   1919: Returned.   09.1924: Sold to Charles Dobson, Grimsby.
12.07.1940: Sunk by enemy aircraft bombs when fishing 10 miles east of Hvalbam, Iceland. Thirteen saved, skipper lost.
29.10.1940: Grimsby registry closed.

NIZAM	386	225	127.0	C D Holmes	Grimsby Union Steam
125047 Steam trawler	20.10.1906	107	22.0	75 rhp 3-cyl	Fishing Co Ltd,
GY231	27.02.1907		11.6	10.5 knots	Grimsby

19.02.1907: Registered at Grimsby (GY231). 1908: Renamed **UGADALE** (GY231).
04.1913: Sold to Anchor Steam Fishing Co Ltd, Grimsby. 14.05.1913: Renamed **MONIMUS** (GY231).
12.01.1914: Posted missing whilst on a North Sea trip. No survivors. 11.02.1914: Grimsby registry closed.

PRESIDENT	387	257	128.0	C D Holmes	Anchor Steam Fishing
125052 Steam trawler	20.11.1906	109	22.0	75 rhp 3-cyl	Co Ltd,
GY262	25.03.1907		11.6	10.5 knots	Grimsby

23.03.1907: Registered at Grimsby (GY262). 03.1907: Sold to James Methven, Grimsby.
12.1914: Requisitioned for war service (1-12pdr) (Ad.No.721). 02.1915: Renamed **PRESIDENCY**.
20.04.1915: Registered as **PRESIDENCY** (GY262). 1919: Returned.
07.1920: Sold to Cia Nacional de Nav Costeira, Rio de Janeiro, Brazil. 14.07.1920: Grimsby registry closed.
1922: Renamed **SANTA MARIA**. Re-measured to 275grt, 109net. 1924: Sold to the Brazilian Government, Rio de Janeiro.
1935: Sold to Cia Nacional de Nav Costeira, Rio de Janeiro. 1949: Sold to shipbreakers and broken up.

CARLTON	388	267	130.6	C D Holmes	Thomas C & F Moss,
125057 Steam trawler	18.12.1906	124	22.0	69 rhp 3-cyl	Grimsby
GY270	26.04.1907		12.1	10.5 knots	

25.04.1907: Registered at Grimsby (GY270). 12.1915: Requisitioned for war service as a minesweeper (1-3pdr) (Ad.No.1965).
21.02.1916: Mined off Folkestone (mine laid on 20.02.1916 by UC.6). Ty/Skipper Joseph H Sandford, RNR, and seven crew lost.
15.03.1916: Grimsby registry closed.

BOMBAY	389	229	120.0	C D Holmes	Grant & Baker Steam
125051 Steam trawler	03.11.1906	116	22.0	70 rhp 3-cyl	Fishing Co Ltd,
GY247	14.03.1907		11.5	10.5 knots	Grimsby

14.03.1907: Registered at Grimsby (GY247). 09.1915: Requisitioned for war service (1-3pdr, 1-2pdr) (Ad.No.1890).
1919: Returned. 06.08.1929: Sold to Diamonds Steam Fishing Co Ltd, Grimsby.
29.11.1939: Requisitioned for war service as a minesweeper; hire rate £57.5.0d per month. 17.02.1940: Returned.
03.08.1942: On an Icelandic trip, sunk at 1654 by torpedo from U-boat (U605) in approximate position 62°N 18°W, no warning given,
all 13 crew lost. 05.08.1942: Reported missing. 23.7.1943: Grimsby registry closed.

NORA NIVEN	390	166	96.0	Great Central Co-op	Napier Fish Supply Co,
121589 Steam trawler	17.11.1906	66	20.6	55 rhp 3-cyl	Napier, New Zealand
	21.01.1907		10.3	10.0 knots	

Designed for conversion to dry cargo. Fitted with refrigeration and ice making equipment by Linde British Refrigeration Co Ltd,
London. 26.05.1907: Registered at Napier. 1908: Sold to New Zealand Trawling & Fish Supply Co Ltd, Napier. Took part in early
fishery research for the New Zealand Government and eventually surveyed the entire coast of both islands.
1932: Sold to New Zealand Fisheries Co Ltd, Napier.
10.1942: Commissioned in RNZN as dan layer (P. No. T23). Served with the 30th Trawler Group.
1944: Sold to National Mortgage & Agency Co of New Zealand, Dunedin. 1947: Sold to shipbreakers and broken up.

CLEON	391	266	128.6	Great Central Co-op	Orient Steam Fishing
125050 Steam trawler	17.01.1907	120	22.0	76 rhp 3-cyl	Co Ltd,
GY240	09.03.1907		11.6	10.5 knots	Grimsby

13.03.1907: Registered at Grimsby (GY240). 05.1915: Requisitioned for war service as a minesweeper (1-3pdr) (Ad.No.1514).
01.02.1918: Mined off Folkestone Gate Buoy. Ty/Skipper Peter C Sinclair, RNR, and eleven crew lost.
16.04.1919: Grimsby registry closed.

WASHINGTON	392	264	125.0	C D Holmes	Premier Steam Fishing
125054 Steam trawler	17.12.1906	121	22.0	70 rhp 3-cyl	Co Ltd,
GY261	09.04.1907		11.7	10.5 knots	Grimsby

09.04.1907: Registered at Grimsby (GY261). 22.12.1908: Stranded near Selvog, Iceland.
16.01.1909: Grimsby registry closed - "Wrecked".

ORLANDO	393	276	128.0	Amos & Smith	Dolphin Steam Fishing
125055 Steam trawler	14.02.1907	124	22.0	70 rhp 3-cyl	Co Ltd,
GY248	18.04.1907		13.0	10.5 knots	Grimsby

16.04.1907: Registered at Grimsby (GY248). 08.1914: Requisitioned for war service as a minesweeper (Ad.No.365).
14.03.1915: Stranded near Stornoway, Lewis. 29.05.1915: Grimsby registry closed - "Stranded".

VIDONIA	394	276	128.0	Amos & Smith	Arctic Steam Fishing
125059 Steam trawler	14.02.1907	124	22.0	70 rhp 3-cyl	Co Ltd,
GY257	10.05.1907		13.0	10.5 knots	Grimsby

10.05.1907: Registered at Grimsby (GY257). 12.1914: Requisitioned for war service as a minesweeper (1-12pdr) (Ad.No.10). 1919:
Returned. 07.1920: Sold to Lindsey Steam Fishing Co Ltd, Grimsby. 01.1943: Sold to Charleston-Smith Trawlers Ltd / Henriksen
&Co Ltd / Newington Steam Trawling Co Ltd / West Dock Steam Fishing Co Ltd, Hull.
13.01.1943: Grimsby registry closed. 18.01.1943: Registered at Hull (H38). 05.06.1940: Requisitioned for war service as an
auxiliary patrol vessel (P. No. 4.33); hire rate £69.0.0d per month. 25.02.1943: Employed on miscellaneous naval duties.
04.1943: Converted to a fuel carrier (Esso), (P. No. Y.712). 06.1944: At Normandy Landings Force G.
07.10.1944: Foundered in English Channel following collision. Seven crew lost. 10.1944: Hull registry closed.

LEANDER 125061　Steam trawler GY260	395 16.02.1907 01.06.1907	276 124	128.0 22.0 13.0	Amos & Smith 70 rhp　3-cyl 10.5 knots	Lindsey Steam Fishing Co Ltd, Grimsby

03.06.1907: Registered at Grimsby (GY260).　08.1914: Requisitioned for war service as a minesweeper (Ad No.18).
02 1915: Renamed **LEANDROS**.　06.08.1915: Mined off Knock Light Buoy; mine laid on 03.08.1915 by UC.5. Seven crew lost.
02.12.1915: Grimsby registry closed.

MARCELLE 　　　Steam trawler O83	396 02.03.1907 31.07.1907	219 88	120.0 21.5 12.0	C D Holmes 74 rhp　3-cyl 10.5 knots	Société Anonyme des Pêcheries Ostendaises, Ostend, Belgium

07.1907: Registered at Ostend (O83).　1910: Sold to Soc Anon Pêcheries à Vapeur, Ostend.
30.01.1917: Stopped by U-boat (U55) off Trevose Head in approximate position 50° 45'N 05° 30'W and sunk by gunfire.
02.1917: Ostend registry closed.

RUBY 121615　Steam trawler M204	397 19.12.1906 26.03.1907	275 104	125.0 22.5 11.9	Amos & Smith 83 rhp　3-cyl 11.0 knots	Robert Cole, Erel E Carter & Barnard H Galvin, Milford Haven

13.03.1907: Registered at Milford (M204).　17.02.1910: Sold to Robert Cole, Erel E Carter, Milford Haven, and David G Jones,
Pembroke Dock.　12.10.1911: Sold to David G Jones, Pembroke Dock, & Robert Cole, Milford Haven.
04.1914: Sold to John E Rushworth, Grimsby, & Herbert Lee, Wimbledon.　06.04.1914: Milford registry closed.
08.04.1914: Registered at Grimsby (GY58).　08.05.1914: Renamed **IDA ADAMS** (GY58).
08.1914: Requisitioned for war service as a minesweeper (1-4", 1-7,5" A/S Howitzer) (Ad.No.252).
02.1916: Sold to Rushworth Steam Fishing Co Ltd, Grimsby.　22.07.1917: Sold to Noah Ashworth & Ernest Tomlinson, Fleetwood.
1919: Returned.　18.07.1919: Grimsby registry closed.　20.07.1919: Registered at Fleetwood (FD327).
02.09.1919: Sold to Vulcan Steam Fishing Co Ltd, Fleetwood.　23.03.1925: Sold to Ernest Noble, Fleetwood.
1926: Sold to Fleetwood Fish Selling Co Ltd, Fleetwood.　18.09.1930: Fishing 9 miles from Barra Head, on hauling warps fouled
lower part of stern casting at rudder pintle. Put into Oban for repair.
21.11.1930: Left Oban in thick fog and stranded on Fisherman's Rock, NW of Portnahaven, Rinns of Islay. Despite crew effort,
flooded and was abandoned, subsequently sinking after slipping off rocks. All crew rescued.　28.11.1930: Fleetwood registry closed.

VINE 125809　Steam drifter BF886	398 18.03.1907 08.06.1907	95 21	86.0 18.5 8.8	Great Central Co-op 40 rhp　2-cyl 9.5 knots	Thompson & Murray, Buckie

06.1907: Registered at Banff (BF886).　1907: Sold to J Nicol, George Nicol, F Nicol, Gardenstown, and others, Banff.
08.1915: Requisitioned for war service as an anti submarine net drifter (1-3pdr) (P. No. 2703).　1920: Returned.
1922: Sold to W Reid & J Simpson, Buckie. Banff registry closed. Registered at Buckie (BCK412).
1925: Sold to W Hay & J Reid, Buckie.　1937: Sold to shipbreakers and broken up.　1938: Buckie registry closed.

LORD CLAUD HAMILTON 124430　Steam drifter LT1047	399 16.03.1907 26.04.1907	81 16	82.0 18.2 8.6	Crabtree & Co 30 rhp　2-cyl 9.0 knots	Lowestoft Steam Herring Drifters Co Ltd, Lowestoft

18.04.1907: Registered at Lowestoft (LT1047).　12.1914: Requisitioned for war service as a patrol boat / minesweeper (1-6pdr)
(Ad.No.1296). Based Ramsgate.　1919: Returned.　04.1926: Sold to J Geddes, Buckie.　21.04.1926: Lowestoft registry closed.
Registered at Buckie (BCK435).　1936: Sold to shipbreakers and broken up.　Buckie registry closed.

LORD CHARLES BERESFORD 124429　Steam drifter LT1046	400 16.03.1907 26.04.1907	81 16	82.0 18.3 8.6	Crabtree & Co 30 rhp　2-cyl 9.0 knots	Lowestoft Steam Herring Drifters Co Ltd, Lowestoft

18.04.1907: Registered at Lowestoft (LT1047).　12.1914: Requisitioned for war service as a patrol / escort vessel (1-6pdr)
(Ad.No.1304). Based Ramsgate.　1919: Returned.　04.1926: Sold to P Coull, Buckie.　21.04.1926: Lowestoft registry closed.
Registered at Buckie (BCK265).　1936: Sold to shipbreakers and broken up.　Buckie registry closed.

PEKEN 127823　Steam trawler GY354	401 07.12.1907 16.01.1908	228 119	120.0 22.0 11.4	C D Holmes 66 rhp　3-cyl 10.0 knots	Henry L Taylor, Grimsby

17.01.1908: Registered at Grimsby (GY354).　08.1914: Requisitioned for war service as a minesweeper (1-6pdrHA) (Ad.No.24).
1919: Returned.　10.1922: Sold to Diamonds Steam Fishing Co Ltd, Grimsby.　04.07.1940: Requisitioned for war service as a
minesweeper (P. No. FY.1821); hire rate £57.0.0d per month.　Based Swansea with M/S Group 145.　13.08.1945: Returned.
1958: Sold to Jacques Bakker & Zonen, Bruges, for breaking up.　19.03.1958: Arrived Bruges.

SOUTHWARD 125070　Steam trawler GY288	402 28.05.1907 28.08.1907	225 121	120.0 22.0 11.4	C D Holmes 70 rhp　3-cyl 10.5 knots	Forward Steam Fishing Co Ltd, Grimsby

28.08.1907: Registered at Grimsby (GY288).　1917: Requisitioned for Fishery Reserve.
01.03.1919: Posted missing (presumed sunk by mine) whilst returning from a Færoes trip. No survivors.
10.04.1919: Grimsby registry closed - "Vessel mined".

Onward (427)

(Authors' collection)

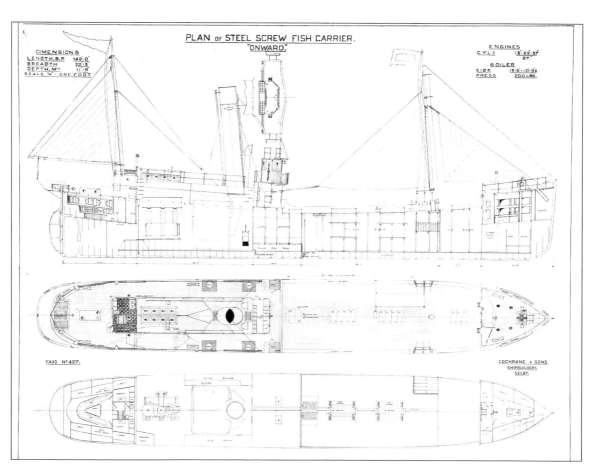

A general arrangement drawing of **Onward**

ONWARD	427	266	142.4	C D Holmes	Great Northern Steamship
124818 Fish carrier/Steam	04.03.1908	112	22.2	98 rhp 3-cyl	Fishing Co Ltd,
H980 trawler	02.04.1908		12.3	11.0 knots	Hull

01.04.1908: Registered at Hull (H980).   12.1914: Requisitioned for war service as a minesweeper (1-12pdr) (Ad.No.399).
11.07.1916: Stopped by U-boat (U52) off Aberdeen, crew taken as prisoners of war. Sunk by gunfire.
26.01.1917: Hull registry closed - "Total loss whilst on Admiralty service".

XERXES	428	243	125.0	C D Holmes	Hector Steam Fishing
124727 Steam trawler	08.03.1908	96	22.0	80 rhp 3-cyl	Co Ltd,
SA55	25.05.1908		11.6	10.5 knots	Swansea

28.05.1908: Registered at Swansea (SA55).   28.01.1913: Sold to Frank Buckworth, Cork, Co Cork.
15.05.1913: Sold to Buckworth & Murphy Ltd, Cork, Co Cork.
12.1914: Requisitioned for war service as a minesweeper (1-6pdr) (Ad.No.835).
16.11.1915: Foundered off Girdle Ness following collision. One casualty.   14.10.1916: Swansea registry closed.

SUSSEX COUNTY	429	84	83.0	Crabtree & Co	Wilfred George Lucas,
127599 Steam drifter	08.03.1908	40	18.0	32 nhp 2-cyl	Lowestoft
LT63	29.04.1908		8.4	9.5 knots	

02.05.1908: Registered at Lowestoft (LT63).   06.07.1908: Sold to County Fishing Co Ltd, Lowestoft.
09.1914: Requisitioned for war service. Sold to The Admiralty. Retained Port Letter Number (LT63) and employed as a
minesweeper / patrol vessel (1-6pdr) (Ad.No.204).   15.09.1921: Sold to County Fishing Co Ltd, Lowestoft.
30.11.1939: Requisitioned for war service employed on contraband control; hire rate £25.0.0d per month.
11.1941: Employed mine watching.   07.1943: Employed on miscellaneous naval duties.   17.04.1945: Returned.
17.07.1946: Sold to Norway.   19.07.1946: Lowestoft registry closed.   29.07.1946: Sailed Lowestoft for Norway.
03.1947: Sold to Alfred Mørch, Vedavågen/Bergen. Renamed **SYDHOLM**. Converted to motor vessel; engine details unknown.
07.1947: Sold to P/R Sydholm (Otto Nakken, Ålesund), Bergen.   1948: Renamed **NØRVØY**.
09.1950: Sold to Petter Myklebust, Fonnes/Bergen.   09.1951: Renamed **TRYGGEN**.
09.1965: Sold to Edvard & Bjarne Drågen, Ersholmen/Bergen.   06.1971: Sold to John & Arne Olsen Hunnestad P/R, Rørvik/Bergen.
04.02.1973: Capsized and sank at Folla.

VIVO	430	270	130.0	Amos & Smith	Mount Steam Fishing
127563 Steam trawler	02.05.1908	103	23.0	88 rhp 3-cyl	Co Ltd,
FD220	11.08.1908		12.2	10.5 knots	Fleetwood

11.08.1908: Registered at Fleetwood.   21.08.1910: Homeward from St Kilda grounds entered thick fog bank in North Channel,
stranded 3½ miles NW of Mull of Galloway. Eleven crew and two trippers picked up by NEW CROWN (GY369) (238grt/1908) and
landed at Drummore.   11.1910: Declared a total loss but attended by Liverpool & Glasgow Salvage Association's steam derrick
barge LADY KATE (135grt/1881) and much equipment and material salvaged.   07.11.1910: Fleetwood registry closed.

PREMIER	431	253	127.0	C D Holmes	Anchor Steam Fishing
127834 Steam trawler	30.05.1908	98	22.0	70 rhp 3-cyl	Co Ltd,
GY385	30.07.1908		11.5	10.5 knots	Grimsby

29.07.1908: Registered at Grimsby (GY385).   09.1914: Requisitioned for war service as a minesweeper (1-6pdr HA) (Ad.No.514).
1919: Returned.   10.02.1923: At 0818 stranded near Robin Hoods Bay, Yorkshire. After salvage attempts failed the nine crew were
taken off by lifeboat. Vessel broke up in heavy seas.   26.02.1923: Grimsby registry closed - "Total wreck".

VARONIL	432	253	127.0	C D Holmes	Atlas Steam Fishing
127835 Steam trawler	16.06.1908	98	22.0	70 rhp 3-cyl	Co Ltd,
GY386	27.08.1908		12.3	10.5 knots	Grimsby

27.08.1908: Registered at Grimsby (GY386).   20.01.1913: Stranded near Grindavik, Iceland.
20.02.1913: Grimsby registry closed.

NORFOLK COUNTY	433	83	84.0	Crabtree & Co	County Fishing Co Ltd,
127618 Steam drifter	16.05.1908	35	18.0	32 nhp 3-cyl	Lowestoft
LT103	06.07.1908			9.5 knots	

09.07.1908: Registered at Lowestoft (LT103).
09.1915: Requisitioned for war service as an anti-submarine net drifter (1-3pdr AA) (Ad.No.2219).   1919: Returned.
29.11.1939: Requisitioned for war service employed on contraband control; hire rate £25.0.0d per month.
08.1943: Employed on miscellaneous naval duties.   17.01.1946: Returned.
11.07.1946: Sold to Hoskul Halvorsen, Arehamn, Norway.   04.07.1946: Lowestoft registry closed.
21.07.1946: Sailed Lowestoft for Norway.   08.08.1946: Registered at Kopervik (R.231).   08.1945: Renamed **SJODRAAT** (R.231).
1948: Converted to motor – 160bhp GM diesel by Kvernenes Skipsbyggeri, Brandasund; new boatdeck fitted; used for fishing and
coasting.   1962: Sold to Mandium Skimmerland, Mosterhamn. Fishing register closed, registered at Haugesund as a coaster.
1966: Re-engined with 160bhp Wichmann diesel (built 1952).   08.1967: Sold to Johannes Skaten, Obnarheim.
1969: Sold to Osvald Kallestad, Stamneshella; registered Bergen, used as a sand carrier.
11.1977: Sold to Richard Veland, Andvikgrend; still used as sand carrier.
2000: Sold to Tim Carter, Manchester, for use as a live aboard.   2004: Sold to Michael Burnett and renamed **NORFOLK COUNTY**.
12.2009: At Port Launay, France, and offered for sale.   2011: Sold to Agge Wendt.

DELTA B	434	220	120.0	Earle's S B & Eng	A Golder & B Brieux,
Steam trawler	16.08.1908	75	21.5	72 nhp 3-cyl	Ostend, Belgium
O171	12.09.1908		11.6	10.5 knots	

19.09.1908: Registered at Ostend (O171).   1910: Sold to Soc Anon 'Delta', Ostend.
09.1914: Escaped from Belgium with refugees and fishing families.   10.1914: At Folkestone with bows damaged.
18.10.1914: Arrived Milford and laid up.   05.1915: Repaired at Swansea and returned to fishing (Skipper Pierre Titeljon).
02.06.1915: Stopped by U-boat (U34) while fishing 12 miles SSW of Scilly Isles, shelled and then skipper forced to place explosive charges. Crew of ten took to boat and later picked up by HM Trawler **DEWSLAND** (M220) (Ad.No.2664) (see Yard No. 421) which landed them at St Mary's, Scilly Isles. Ostend registry closed.

Un-named	435		46.0	N/A	Thomas Wilson Sons & Co Ltd (Wilson Line), Hull
Lighter	26.09.1908		16.0		

Un-named	436		46.0	N/A	Thomas Wilson Sons & Co Ltd (Wilson Line), Hull
Lighter	26.09.1908		16.0		

Un-named	437		46.0	N/A	Thomas Wilson Sons & Co Ltd (Wilson Line), Hull
Lighter	26.09.1908		16.0		

Un-named	438		46.0	N/A	Thomas Wilson Sons & Co Ltd (Wilson Line), Hull
Lighter	26.09.1908		16.0		

CONSORT	439	157	94.0	Crabtree & Co	J Constant,
Steam tug	10.09.1908	21	23.0	28 nhp 2-cyl x 2	London
	25.09.1908		9.6	10 knots	

1909: Sold to S Pearson & Son Ltd, London.   1912: Sold to Port of Pará Co, Pará, Brazil. Renamed **PARREIROS HORTA**.
1956: Reported as non-seagoing and removed from Lloyd's Register of Shipping.

Un-named	440		46.0	N/A	Thomas Wilson Sons & Co Ltd (Wilson Line), Hull
Lighter	30.12.1908		16.0		

Un-named	441		46.0	N/A	Thomas Wilson Sons & Co Ltd (Wilson Line), Hull
Lighter	30.12.1908		16.0		

Un-named	442		46.0	N/A	Thomas Wilson Sons & Co Ltd (Wilson Line), Hull
Lighter	30.12.1908		16.0		

Un-named	443		46.0	N/A	Thomas Wilson Sons & Co Ltd (Wilson Line), Hull
Lighter	30.12.1908		16.0		

ESPERANTO	444	217	115.2	Crabtree & Co	Joseph H Beckwith,
125752 Steam coaster	12.10.1908	81	22.1	33 rhp 3-cyl	Colchester
	19.12.1908		8.1	9.5 knots	

02.01.1908: Registered at London: 10.1911: New boiler fitted. 1926: Sold to John Taylor & Son, Sunderland. Renamed **ELEMORE**.
1927: Sold to T Small & Co (Gt Yarmouth) Ltd, Great Yarmouth. Renamed **NORWICH TRADER**.
1932: Sold to Gt. Yarmouth Shipping Co Ltd, Great Yarmouth.   06.01.1942: Mined on passage London towards Great Yarmouth with general cargo and foundered in approximate position 51 55 07 N 01 32 05 E. Six crew and one gunner were lost.
07 - 12.1943: Wreck dispersed.

ROSE OF ENGLAND	445	223	120.2	C D Holmes	Joseph Duncan,
127954 Steam trawler	09.11.1908	86	22.0	68 rhp 3-cyl	Liverpool
LL6	09.01.1908			10.5 knots	

07.01.1909: Registered at Liverpool (LL6).   01.1915: Requisitioned for war service as a minesweeper (1-6pdr HA) (Ad.No.507).
1919: Returned.   12.1935: Sold to W Franklin, Grimsby.   18.12.1935: Liverpool registry closed.
19.12.1935: Registered at Grimsby (GY236).
27.11.1939: Requisitioned for war service as a minesweeper; hire rate £55.15.0d per month.   29.01.1940: Returned.
17.09.1940: Requisitioned for war service as a minesweeper (P. No. FY.562). Based Grimsby with the M/S Groups 110 and 72.
28.01.1946: Returned.   1961: Sold to Van Heyghen Frères, Bruges, for breaking up.   16.11.1961: Arrived Bruges.
11.1961: Grimsby registry closed.

SCOMBER 127572　Steam trawler FD90	446 24.12.1908 06.03.1909	270 102	130.0 23.0 12.2	C D Holmes 76 rhp　3-cyl 10.5 knots	Mount Steam Fishing Co Ltd, Fleetwood

03.03.1909: Registered at Fleetwood (FD90).　1914: Sold to Galiana y del Valles Trillo S en C, Barcelona.
15.05.1914: Fleetwood registry closed.　Registered at Barcelona.
1918: Sold to Government of France, Paris, (Transports Maritimes et Marine Marchande). Renamed **ANNIBAL**.
1922: Sold to Victor Bosquet, La Rochelle. Renamed **NEPTUNE I** (LR2534).
1934: Sold to 'Sorima' Soc Ricuperi Marittimi, Genoa, Italy. Renamed **RAMPINO**. Converted to a salvage vessel; tonnages now
301grt, 112net.　01.1942: War loss.　1943: Salvaged and broken up.

NOTRE DAME DES DUNES 　　　Steam trawler B84	447 25.01.1909 20.03.1909	482 103	160.0 25.0 13.6	Amos & Smith 75 nhp　3-cyl 10.5 knots	Vve Christiaens & A Bourgain, Boulogne, France

1927: Sold to Christiaens Fils & Co, Boulogne.　1930: Sold to Pêcheries de la Morinie, Boulogne.
25.05.1940: Sunk by enemy aircraft during the Dunkirk evacuation.

CLAUDIUS 127840　Steam trawler GY409	448 06.02.1909 06.04.1909	285 126	136.7 23.0 12.1	Amos & Smith 87 rhp　3-cyl 10.5 knots	Consolidated Steam Fishing & Ice Co Ltd, Grimsby

07.04.1909: Registered at Grimsby (GY409).　12.1913: Sold to Reunion Steam Fishing Co Ltd, Grimsby.
20.12.1913: Renamed **TATIANA** (GY977).　18.11.1914: Sold to South Western Steam Fishing Co Ltd, Grimsby and Fleetwood.
03.1915: Sold to A Bannister, Grimsby.　31.07.1916: Stopped by U-boat (UB39) when fishing 36 miles SE by E from Tyne piers;
sunk. All crew took to boat.　15.08.1916: Grimsby registry closed - "Sunk by submarine".

DIPLOMAT 128130　Steam tug	449 24.12.1908 18.02.1909	91	83.0 17.0 9.7	Earle's SB & Eng 48 rhp　2-cyl 10.0 knots	Thomas Clarkson Spink, Hull

18.02.1909: Registered at Hull.　15.02.1915: Vessel posted missing.　10.03.1915: Hull registry closed.

HALLER 129243　Steam coaster	450 05.06.1909 19.08.1909	679 283	178.0 30.0 12.3	C D Holmes 93 rhp　3-cyl 10.5 knots	George R Haller Ltd, Hull

24.08.1909: Registered at Hull.　10.01.1919: Sold to Dundee Perth & London Shipping Co Ltd, Dundee.
19.05.1919: Hull registry closed.　1920: Renamed **GOWRIE**. Registered at Dundee. Tonnages re-measured to 689grt, 285net.
09.01.1945: On passage from Aberdeen towards Hull, foundered after attack by enemy aircraft four miles east of Stonehaven. All
crew rescued.

CANADA 　　　Steam trawler B90	451 23.02.1909 29.04.1909	486 277	165.0 26.1 12.3	Amos & Smith 113 nhp　3-cyl 11.0 knots	J Huret, Boulogne, France

12.09.1918: Stranded at Agadir, Morocco.　Total loss.

SHOTTON 124624　Steam coaster	452 07.04.1909 27.05.1909	300 110	135.0 23.1 9.3	C D Holmes 62 rhp　2-cyl 10.5 knots	Coppack Brothers & Co, Connah's Quay

1912: Transferred to Thomas Coppack, Connah's Quay.　12.1912: Sold to Shotton Steamship Co Ltd, Ipswich.
10.1916: Sold to Lythgoe Amundsen & Co, Sunderland.　1918: Sold to James Lythgoe & Co, Sunderland.
1919: Sold to R & D A Duncan Ltd, Belfast.　08.1919: Renamed **TORYISLAND**.　1926: Sold to William Carney, Sunderland.
02.1938: Sold to Sir James Laing & Sons Ltd, Sunderland.　06.1940: Sold to Efford Shipping Co Ltd, London.
1946: Renamed **SPRINGFIELD**.　04.1948: Sold to I P Langford (Shipping) Ltd, Sharpness. Renamed **CHRISTINA DAWN**.
03.04.1949: In strong winds driven ashore in Irvine harbour having arrived from Port Talbot with carbide in drums.
14.04.1949: With damage to bottom plates and ingress of water, cargo exploded with resultant fire.
15.04.1949: Explosions ceased.　Subsequently declared a total loss.

ELITE 　　Grand Bank Salter PLN unknown	453 22.04.1909 07.07.1909	487 305	160.0 27.0 12.3	Amos & Smith 117 nhp　3-cyl 10.75 knots	Parceria Geral de Pescarias, Lisbon, Portugal

1914: Sold to A Castilho, Lisbon; renamed **AUGUSTO DE CASTILHO**.
1914: Requisitioned for war service as a minesweeper in Portuguese Navy.　14.10.1918: Escorting Portuguese steamer
SAN MIGUEL (2576grt/1905) from Madeira to Azores, attacked by U-boat (U139) 100 miles SW of Azores. Engaged enemy but was
sunk with four casualties from crew of forty-two. SAN MIGUEL escaped to Ponte Delgada.

Arian (466)

(Authors' collection)

S. L. Haldane (468)

(Barnard & Straker collection)

H. A. L. Russell (469)

(Jonathan Grobler collection)

PRINCE VICTOR	470	207	115.2	C D Holmes	A Cook,
127865 Steam trawler	07.07.1910	94	21.5	65 rhp 3-cyl	Grimsby
GY569	16.08.1910		11.5	10.5 knots	

12.08.1910: Registered at Grimsby (GY569).   11.1910: Sold to Henry Bernstein, Grimsby.
04.1915: Requisitioned for war service as a minesweeper (1-6pdr) (Ad.No.1442).
10.07.1917: Sold to Zaree Steam Fishing Co Ltd, Grimsby.   1919: Returned.
11.1923: Sold to Great Central Co-op Eng & Ship Repair Co Ltd, Grimsby.
06.1928: Sold to Trawlers White Sea & Grimsby Ltd, Grimsby.   01.1942: Sold to Trawlers Grimsby Ltd, Grimsby.
28.03.1944: Requisitioned for war service on miscellaneous naval duties; hire rate not recorded.
06.1944: Took part in the D-Day landings as a smoke-making trawler (Group B1).   29.11.1944: Returned.
01.1946: Sold to T C & F Moss Ltd, Grimsby.   03.1956: Sold to Belgium for breaking up.   12.04.1956: Arrived Boom, near Antwerp.
11.1956: Grimsby registry closed.

EILEEN DUNCAN	471	223	120.1	C D Holmes	John Duncan,
131306 Steam trawler	24.08.1910	86	22.0	67 rhp 3-cyl	Liverpool
LL36	28.10.1910		11.5	10.5 knots	

27.10.1910: Registered at Liverpool (LL36).   01.1915: Requisitioned for war service as a minesweeper (1-6pdr HA) (Ad.No.508).
1919: Returned.   07.1936: Sold to William & George R Wood, Aberdeen.   09.07.1936: Liverpool registry closed.
10.07.1936: Registered at Aberdeen (A413).
07.01.1940: Requisitioned for war service as a boom defence trawler; hire rate £55.15.0d per month.   16.01.1940: Returned.
09.07.1940: Requisitioned for war service as a minesweeper. Based North Shields with M/S Group 148.
30.09.1941: Alongside Bergen Wharf, North Shields (T/Lt. G N Ward, RNR). Attacked by enemy aircraft and sunk. Eight crew lost.
STAR OF DEVERON (A55) sunk in same attack.   26.11.1943: Aberdeen registry closed.

WISHFUL	472	83	83.0	Crabtree & Co	Eastern Drifters Co Ltd,
129985 Steam drifter	25.05.1910	35	18.0	32 rhp 3-cyl	Lowestoft
LT661	14.07.1910		8.4	9.5 knots	

14.07.1910: Registered at Lowestoft (LT661).
09.1914: Requisitioned for war service as a minesweeper and anti submarine net drifter (1-6pdr HA) (Ad.No.218).
1918: Sold to Streonshalh Fishing Co Ltd, Whitby.   05.03.1918: Lowestoft registry closed.   03.1918: Registered at Whitby (WY247).
1919: Returned.   1919: Sold to Ramsgate Steam Trawling Co Ltd, Ramsgate. Whitby registry closed. Registered at Ramsgate.
10.02.1921: Foundered in English Channel after being run down by Danish steamer INDIAN (5554grt); eight crew lost including
Skipper Alfred Catt; one survivor, Percy Cowling, picked up.

HULL TRADER	473	304	127.1	Crabtree & Co	Frederick W Horlock,
132230 Steam coaster	17.12.1910	130	22.5	45 nhp 3-cyl	Mistley
	30.02.1911		9.6	8.5 knots	

11.03.1911: Registered at Hull.   13.02.1915: In severe SW gale, foundered 3 miles SW of Dover when her cargo shifted whilst on
passage from Mistley towards Dublin. Three crew managed to get away in boat and were picked up by a warship.
Four crew lost.   04.03.1915: Hull registry closed.

ALBERIA	474	286	130.2	Amos & Smith	Crown Steam Fishing
132091 Steam trawler	07.09.1910	112	23.5	90 rhp 3-cyl	Co Ltd,
GY588	07.11.1910		12.3	10.5 knots	Grimsby

07.11.1910: Registered at Grimsby (GY588).   12.1914: Requisitioned for war service as a minesweeper (1-12pdr, W/T) (Ad.No.768).
1919: Returned.   05.1934: Sold to Mount Steam Fishing Co Ltd, Fleetwood.   08.1934: Sold to Alberic Steam Fishing Co Ltd,
Fleetwood.   10.10.1934: Renamed **ALBERIC** (GY588).   25.04.1940: Requisitioned for war service as a minesweeper; hire rate
£71.10.0d per month. Based at North Shields with M/S Group 63.
03.05.1941: Sunk in accidental collision with destroyer HMS ST ALBANS (P. No. I.15) in Pentland Firth (T/Lt R M Johnson, RNR).
Fourteen crew lost.   06.1941: Grimsby registry closed.

WALLINGTON	475	259	130.3	C D Holmes	Premier Steam Fishing
132095 Steam trawler	18.01.1911	110	22.5	75 rhp 3-cyl	Co Ltd,
GY599	16.02.1911		12.0	10.5 knots	Grimsby

13.02.1911: Registered at Grimsby (GY599).   12.1914: Requisitioned for service as a boom defence vessel (1-6pdr HA).
09.1918: Converted to a minesweeper (1-12pdr).   Renamed **ORIFLAMME** (Ad.No.1659).
1919: Returned and reverted to **WALLINGTON** (GY599).   18.09.1918: Sold to James Coombes, Grimsby.
06.1925: Sold to M Fernandez Pujol, Cadiz, Spain.   29.06.1925: Grimsby registry closed. Renamed **SANTA MARIA P**.
1932: Sold to M Sibon Perinan, Cadiz.   1949: Sold to Rafael Prieto Sancho, Cadiz.
1959: Sold to Dionisio Tejero Perez S A, Corunna.   1966: Sold to shipbreakers and broken up.

APAR	476	91	75.2	Earle's SB & Eng	J Constant,
129137 Steam tug	08.08.1910		21.2	400 ihp 3-cyl	London
	20.09.1910		9.6		

Sold on completion to Gaselee & Son Ltd, London. Registered for towing services on the River Thames.
1914: Requisitioned for war service at Le Havre and Dieppe.   1920: Returned.
06.05.1932: Collided with and slightly damaged Battersea Bridge.   06.04.1938: Collided with the German steam ship NORDMARK
(1060grt/1907) off Surrey Docks, River Thames.   1947: Sold to shipbreakers and broken up.

Balfour (524)

(Barnard & Straker collection)

Bonar Law (525)

(Barnard & Straker collection)

Ploughboy (527)

(George Scales collection)

BALFOUR	524	285	133.5	C D Holmes	Pickering & Haldane's
133388 Steam trawler	04.04.1912	114	23.0	65 rhp 3-cyl	Steam Trawling Co Ltd,
H432	22.06.1912		12.0	10.0 knots	Hull

17.06.1912: Registered at Hull (H432).   02.1915: Requisitioned for war service as a minesweeper (1-3pdr) (Ad.No.1228).
13.05.1918: Foundered following collision with the Royal Sovereign Light Vessel. All crew saved.   15.04.1919: Hull registry closed.

BONAR LAW	525	285	133.5	C D Holmes	Pickering & Haldane's
133389 Steam trawler	20.04.1912	114	23.0	65 rhp 3-cyl	Steam Trawling Co Ltd,
H437	27.06.1912		12.0	10.0 knots	Hull

20.06.1912: Registered at Hull (H437).   02.1915: Requisitioned for war service as a minesweeper (1-3pdr) (Ad.No.1223).
27.10.1915: Foundered following collision with South Goodwin Light Vessel. All crew saved.   15.11.1916: Hull registry closed.

HILDA & ERNEST	526	102	88.0	Crabtree & Co	Ernest V Snowling,
132949 Steam drifter	06.03.1912	47	19.1	35 rhp 2-cyl	Lowestoft
LT1173	26.06.1912		9.0	9.5 knots	

22.08.1912: Registered at Lowestoft (LT1173).   02.1915: Requisitioned for war service as a patrol boat (1-3pdr) (Ad.No.201).
1919: Returned.   1919: Sold to J V Breach, Lowestoft.   01.04.1919: Renamed **BOY NAT** (LT1173).
04.03.1920: Sold to Thanet Steam Trawling Co Ltd, London.   05.03.1920: Lowestoft registry closed. Registered at Ramsgate (R116).
1920: Capsized while coaling in Ramsgate harbour. Subsequently raised and returned to service.
01.1924: Sold to F Spashett, Lowestoft.   01.1924: Ramsgate registry closed.   30.01.1924: Registered at Lowestoft (LT1298).
31.01.1924: Sold to A W Catchpole & C G Allerton, Lowestoft.   04.09.1924: Sold to Hobson & Co (Lowestoft) Ltd, Lowestoft.
23.12.1924: Sold to T A Utting, Lowestoft.   28.02.1925: Renamed **AVAILABLE** (LT1298).
03.05.1926: Sold to J Innes, G Reid, W Smith, J P Buchan & G McWilliam, Buckie.   03.05.1926: Lowestoft registry closed.
05.1926: Registered at Buckie (BCK440).
28.11.1939: Requisitioned for war service on contraband control; hire rate £27.0.0d per month.   25.01.1946: Returned.
1947: Sold to W J McIntosh, Mrs M McIntosh, Peterhead, & others. Buckie registration closed. Registered at Fraserburgh (FR167).
1949: Sold to Thomas Buchan, St Combs & others.   06.1951: Sold to G & W Brunton, Grangemouth, for breaking up.
1951: Fraserburgh registry closed.

PLOUGHBOY	527	102	88.0	Crabtree & Co	Samuel Turrell,
132948 Steam drifter	07.03.1912	47	19.1	35 rhp 2-cyl	Lowestoft
LT1177	06.06.1912		9.0	9.5 knots	

22.05.1912: Registered at Lowestoft (LT1177).   09.1915: Requisitioned for war service as an anti-submarine net drifter (1-3pdr HA)
(Ad.No.1909).   07.03.1919: Sold to Ploughing Co Ltd, Lowestoft.   Post-12.03.1919: Returned to owner.
31.05.1937: Sold to Leonard T J Leftley, Lowestoft.   31.05.1937: Sold to Vigilant Fishing Co Ltd, Lowestoft.
13.11.1939: Requisitioned for war service on examing service/minesweeper duties; hire rate £27.0.0d per month. Based at Malta.
01.03.1941: When off Malta, severely damaged by explosion of three mines in close proximity. One rating killed, nine injured. Vessel
beached.   31.10.1941: Compulsorily acquired by Ministry of War Transport. Salved, repaired and returned to service. Employed
boom working (P. No. Z.303).   07.1946: Sold to shipbreakers and broken up.

EAGER	528	102	88.0	Crabtree & Co	Sidney G Allerton,
132962 Steam drifter	07.03.1912	47	19.1	35 rhp 3-cyl	Lowestoft
LT1166	22.06.1912		9.0	9.5 knots	

20.06.1912: Registered at Lowestoft (LT1166).   08.1914: Requisitioned for war service as a patrol boat (1-6pdr HA) (Ad.No.202).
02.1919: Returned.   1933: Half ownership transferred to Frederick Spashett, Lowestoft.
15.11.1939: Requisitioned for war service as a minesweeper (P. No. FY.990); hire rate £27.13.6d per month. Based Greenock.
04.1944: Employed on port duties.   06.1944: Employed on miscellaneous naval duties in support of Normandy landings.
10.1944: Continued miscellaneous naval duties.   1945: Sold to Bay Fisheries Ltd, Fleetwood.   10.1945: Returned.
1947: Sold to Henry B Roberts, Lowestoft.   1951: Sold to J W Burwood, Lowestoft.   1952: Sold to Eager Fishing Co Ltd, Lowestoft.
1953: Sold to W H Podd Ltd, Lowestoft.   1954: Converted to motor vessel by LBS Engineering Co Ltd, Lowestoft. Re-engined with
300bhp 3-cyl AKD diesel by W H Podd Ltd, Lowestoft.   1954: Sold to Diesel Trawlers Ltd, Lowestoft.
1963: Sold to Gamashie Fishing & Marketing Co, Accra, Ghana.   1972: Sunk.

ANDREW MARVEL	529	285	133.5	C D Holmes	Pickering & Haldane's
133396 Steam trawler	17.06.1912	114	23.0	64 rhp 3-cyl	Steam Trawling Co Ltd,
H466	15.07.1912		12.0	10.0 knots	Hull

11.07.1912: Registered at Hull (H466).   02.1915: Requisitioned for war service as a minesweeper (1-12pdr) (Ad.No.1180).
1919: Returned.   18.08.1919: Sold to Jutland Steam Trawling Co Ltd, Hull.   20.09.1919: Renamed **NAVAL BASE** (H466).
29.05.1920: Sold to Jutland Amalgamated Trawlers Co Ltd, Hull.
08.1925: Sold to Soc Portuense de Pesca D'Arrasto Ltda, Oporto, Portugal.
29.08.1925: Hull registry closed - "On sale of vessel to Portugal".   Renamed **FAFE**.
1963: Continued existence in doubt. Removed from Lloyd's Register of Shipping.

Isa (537)

Silver Line (538)

ISA		537	217	115.0	Earle's SB & Eng	Soc Anon des Pêcheries
	Steam trawler	29.08.1912	100	21.5	70 nhp 3-cyl	à Vapeur,
O81		09.10.1912			10.0 knots	Ostend, Belgium

10.1912: Registered at Ostend.   28.10.1914: Fishing from Milford Haven.
29.05.1917: Requisitioned for Fishery Reserve, with owner's permission.
12.06.1917: On Irish grounds (Capitaine Louis Philippe Dedrie) picked up boat with twenty-three survivors from steamer BAY STATE (6583grt) torpedoed on 10.06 by U66 250 miles NW of Fastnet.
20.06.1917: Picked up eighteen crew members from steamer ENGLISH MONARCH (4947grt/1905) torpedoed on 18.06 by U24 300 miles NW of Fastnet.
02.07.1917: Off Bull Rock picked up twenty-four survivors of Italian steamer PHOEBUS (3133grt/1894) torpedoed on 30.06 by UC44 off Berehaven.   1917: Fitted with 6-pdr gun at Swansea.
04.12.1917: Fishing off the Smalls in company with EMMANUEL (O87), ARIES (M97) and LOLIST (LT427) engaged a submarine with gunfire and pursued for 18 miles.   1919: Released to owner.   04.1930: Sold to Cevic Steam Fishing Co Ltd, Fleetwood.
04.1930: Ostend registry closed.   04.04.1930: Renamed ISER (FD79).
02.1943: Sold to R G Parsley (Don Trawling Co (Milford Haven) Ltd), Milford Haven.
03.1955: Sold to BISCO and allocated to Thos W Ward Ltd, Sheffield, for breaking up at Castle Pill, Milford Haven.
Fleetwood registry closed.

SILVER LINE		538	92	84.5	Crabtree & Co	Ernest Turrell,
132967	Steam drifter	18.05.1912	42	18.5	33 ihp 2-cyl	Kessingland
LT1179		20.07.1912		9.0	9.5 knots	

18.07.1912: Registered at Lowestoft (LT1179).
09.1914: Requisitioned for war service as a patrol boat/minesweeper (1-3pdr) (Ad.No.217).   1919: Returned.
29.10.1919: Sold to Lion Fishing Co Ltd, Lowestoft.
3.3.1922: Sold to William Jenkinson Watkinson & Robert Watkinson, Filey, for long lining and seining.
27.02.1935: Lowestoft registry closed.   04.03.1935: Registered at Scarborough (SH50).
11.10.1946: Sold to Frederick William Monkman, Scarborough.   03.05.1947: Sold to Iris Fishing Co Ltd, Scarborough.
1952: Sold to Northern Shipbreaking Co Ltd, Peterhead, for breaking up. Sold to Metal Industries (Salvage) Ltd, Glasgow, and allocated to Charlestown, Fife, for breaking up.   26.06.1952: Arrived Charlestown.   01.07.1952: Breaking commenced.   04.09.1952: Scarborough registry closed.

LUNEDA		539	288	130.0	C D Holmes	Lancashire Steam Fishing
132412	Steam trawler	14.09.1912	116	23.0	65 rhp 3-cyl	Co Ltd,
FD230		07.11.1912		12.7	10.0 knots	Fleetwood

08.11.1912: Registered at Fleetwood (FD230).
11.1914: Requisitioned for war service as a minesweeper (1-12pdr, 1-7.5" A/S Howitzer) (Ad.No.926).   1919: Returned.
02.06.1920: Sold to J Marr & Son Ltd, Fleetwood.
08.02.1937: Sailed Fleetwood for west of Scotland grounds (Skipper Richard Snape).   09.01.1937: In the early hours approaching Islay, in snow storm with zero visibility and heavy swell, struck rocks off Ardbeg, offshore of Carmichael's Rock. Attempts to refloat failed and with forepeak flooded and listing, twelve crew took to lifeboat, picked up by the puffer PIBROCH (96grt/1923) and landed at Port Ellen.   24.02.1937: Fleetwood registry closed.

INGOLFUR ARNARSON		540	306	135.0	Amos & Smith	P J Thorsteinsson,
	Steam trawler	17.07.1912	141	23.5	88 nhp 3-cyl	Reykjavik, Iceland
RE153		10.10.1912		12.6	10.5 knots	

10.1912: Registered at Reykjavik (RE153).   1915: Sold to Fiskveidafelaginu Haukum, Reykjavik.
1917: Sold to René Petit, Dieppe, France, and renamed SINGE and registered at Dieppe.
10.1924: Sold to Consolidated Steam Fishing & Ice Co (Grimsby) Ltd, Grimsby. Dieppe registry closed.
22.10.1924: Renamed NEBRIS (GY84).   09.1927: Owners re-styled Consolidated Fisheries Ltd, Grimsby.
04.1937: Sold at Grimsby to Metal Industries Ltd, Glasgow, for £1136 and allocated to Rosyth for breaking up.
05.1937: Arrived Rosyth.   08.05.1937: Grimsby registry closed.   26.05.1937: Breaking commenced.

ÆGIR		541	244	119.1	C D Holmes	D Hurtley & Sons Ltd,
133416	Steam coaster	28.09.1912	95	23.5	47 rhp 2-cyl	Hull
		30.11.1912		8.2	10.0 knots	

27.11.1912: Registered at Hull.   07.01.1918: Sold to Co-operative Wholesale Society Ltd, Manchester.
30.10.1924: Sold to G T Gillie & Blair Ltd, Newcastle.   04.11.1924: Sold to Société Etaploise de Transport Maritime, Etaples, France. Renamed VILLE D'ETAPLES.   04.11.1924: Hull registry closed.   02.1926: Sold to James Davies, Cardigan. Renamed TEIFI. Registered at Cardigan.   10.11.1930: On passage from Cardigan towards Cardiff in ballast, struck submerged object off Flat Holm, Bristol Channel, and foundered in position 51° 23.27'N 03° 08.02' W.

BALSENSE		542	48	68.5	Crabtree & Co	Balsense No Algarve,
	Pilchard fisher	02.07.1912	21	17.5	22 nhp 2-cyl	Tavira, Portugal
		01.08.1912			9.0 knots	

No further details.

Clotilde (579)

(Authors'collection)

T. R. Ferens (580)

(Barnard & Straker collection)

Beryl (583)

(Barnard & Straker collection)

CLOTILDE	579	289	130.2	C D Holmes	J Marr & Son Ltd,
132418 Steam trawler	04.09.1913	114	25.5	84 rhp 3-cyl	Fleetwood
FD232	02.12.1913		12.6	10.5 knots	

26.11.1913: Registered at Fleetwood (FD232).   11.1914: Requisitioned for war service as a minesweeper (1-6pdr) (Ad.No.924).
1919: Returned.   15.08.1919: Sold to Active Fishing Co Ltd, Fleetwood.
29.02.1940: Requisitioned for war service as a minesweeper (P. No. FY.534). Based Yarmouth with M/S Group 13.
25.11.1944: Sold to Wembley Steam Fishing Co (Grimsby) Ltd, Grimsby.   12.1945: Returned.
22.10.1946: Fleetwood registry closed.   10.1946: Registered at Grimsby (GY352).
11.1947: Sold to Dinas Steam Trawling Co Ltd, Fleetwood.   04.1952: Sold to Queen Steam Fishing Co Ltd, Grimsby.
12.1956: Sold to Leon Engelen, Willebroek, Belgium, for demolition.   03.12.1956: Breaking commenced.   Grimsby registry closed.

T. R. FERENS	580	307	136.7	Amos & Smith	Pickering & Haldane's
136165 Steam trawler	02.10.1913	124	23.2	93 rhp 3-cyl	Steam Trawling Co Ltd,
H1027	29.11.1913		12.3	10.0 knots	Hull

22.11.1913: Registered at Hull (H1027).
05.1915: Requisitioned for war service as a minesweeper (1-12pdr, 1-7.5" A/S Howitzer) (Ad.No.1518).   1919: Returned.
02.1920: Sold to Fiskiveidahutafelagid Hilmir, Reykjavik, Iceland.   23.02.1920: Hull registry closed.
09.03.1920: Renamed **HILMIR** (RE240).   22.03.1922: Sold to Fiskiveidahlutafelaginu Njali, Reykjavik.
09.12.1941: Owners moved to Bildudal.   01.01.1945: Sold to Gunnari Gudjonssyni, Reykjavik. Renamed **KOPANES** (VN25).
02.1947: Sold to P/f Rituvikar Trolarafelag A/S, Ridevig, Færoe Islands. Renamed **SKORAKLETTUR**.
1953: Sold to P/f Var, Vestmanhavn Færoe Islands. Renamed **KOPANES**.
15.05.1955: Struck a rock whilst on passage to Faeringehavn, Greenland. Declared a total loss.

ONYX	581	248	121.9	C D Holmes	Kingston Steam Trawling
136167 Steam trawler	30.10.1913	98	22.1	76 rhp 3-cyl	Co Ltd,
H1029	20.12.1913		12.2	11.0 knots	Hull

18.12.1913: Registered at Hull (H1029).
04.1915: Requisitioned for war service as an escort vessel (1-6pdr, 1-7.5" A/S Howitzer) (Ad.No.1186).
11.05.1915: Renamed **ONYX II**.   14.05.1915: Registered as **ONYX II** (H1029).   1919: Returned.
03.03.1926: Sold to R Hastie, North Shields.   08.03.1926: Hull registry closed.   11.03.1926: Registered at North Shields (SN36).
14.04.1926: Renamed **MARY A. HASTIE** (SN36).   1930: Sold to Vereenigde Exploitatie Maatschappij, IJmuiden, Netherlands.
23.07.1929: North Shields registry closed.   Renamed **AMSTERDAM** (IJM58).
1939: Requisitioned by the Koninklijke Marine as a buoy tender (P. No. 4).
1940: Fitted out as a minesweeper (P. No. FY.1921), RNIN crew.   1941: Renamed **ANDIJK**.
03.1943: Transferred to Netherlands Shipping & Trading Commission, London. RN crew.
20.03.1946: Returned and reverted to **AMSTERDAM** (IJM58).   1946: Sold to Vereenigde Steenkolenhandel V, IJmuiden.
1952: Sold to shipbreakers and broken up.   IJmuiden registry closed.

AGATE	582	248	121.9	C D Holmes	Kingston Steam Trawling
136169 Steam trawler	30.10.1913	98	22.1	76 rhp 3-cyl	Co Ltd,
H2	12.01.1914		12.2	11.0 knots	Hull

05.01.1914: Registered at Hull (H2).   05.1915: Requisitioned for war service as a minesweeper (1-6pdr) (Ad.No.1635).
14.03.1918: Mined off Royal Sovereign Light Vessel; mine laid on same day by UC.71. Four crew lost.
04.06.1918: Hull registry closed - "Lost whilst on Admiralty service".

BERYL	583	248	121.9	C D Holmes	Kingston Steam Trawling
136175 Steam trawler	15.11.1913	98	22.1	76 rhp 3-cyl	Co Ltd,
H31	29.01.1914		12.2	11.0 knots	Hull

27.01.1914: Registered at Hull (H31).   12.1914: Requisitioned for war service as a minesweeper (2-6pdr HA) (Ad.No.1139).
20.03.1915: Renamed **BERYL II**.   17.04.1915: Registered as **BERYL II** (H31).   1919: Returned.
08.12.1926: Sold to Cam & Sons, Sydney, Australia.   16.02.1927: Hull registry closed.   1927: Registered at Sydney.
1934: Company re-styled Cam & Sons Ltd, Sydney, Australia.
09.1939: Requisitioned for war service in Royal Australian Navy as a minesweeper (P. No. FY.71).
1944: Employed as boom gate vessel (P. No. Z.101).   1946: Returned to Cam & Sons Pty Ltd, Sydney, Australia.
03.1956: Sold to shipbreakers and broken up.   03.1956: Sydney registry closed.

JACINTH	584	248	121.9	C D Holmes	Kingston Steam Trawling
136181 Steam trawler	29.11.1913	98	22.1	76 rhp 3-cyl	Co Ltd,
H33	24.02.1914		12.2	11.0 knots	Hull

23.02.1914: Registered at Hull (H33).   02.1916: Requisitioned for war service as a minesweeper (1-12pdr, 1-6pdr HA) (Ad.No.1226).
21.08.1917: In Firth of Tay with HM Trawlers THOMAS YOUNG (Ad.No.1143) (SN67) and SHIKARI (Ad.No.67) (GY364) sank U-boat
(UC41) which had suffered damage when minelaying.   1919: Returned.
27.02.1926: Sold to Bunch Steam Fishing Co Ltd, Grimsby.   27.02.1926: Hull registry closed.
05.03.1926: Registered at Grimsby (GY383).   28.11.1928: Sold to David Dryburgh, Newhaven, Edinburgh.   15.09.1934: After
receiving radio message, rescued members of a British Arctic exploration team from Angmagssalik, Greenland, and returned them
safely to Aberdeen.   05.02.1936: Grimsby registry closed.   02.1936: Renamed **INVERFORTH** (GN52).
30.12.1937: Connected to Aberdeen steam trawler CALVINIA (A8) which had lost propeller and delivered her to Aberdeen after 15
mile tow.   28.11.1939: Requisitioned for war service as a minesweeper (P. No. FY.729); hire rate £66.2.8d per month. Based
Swansea with M/S Group 132.   1945: Sold to Yolland Bros Ltd, Milford Haven.   12.04.1946: Returned.
1946: Sold to Cairo Fishing Co, Milford Haven.   1955: Sold to Belgian shipbreakers.
16.08.1955: Arrived Ruisbroek for breaking up.   08.1955: Granton registry closed.

Index of vessel names following sale or transfer (and yard number)